Entropy

Ravven White

Entropy

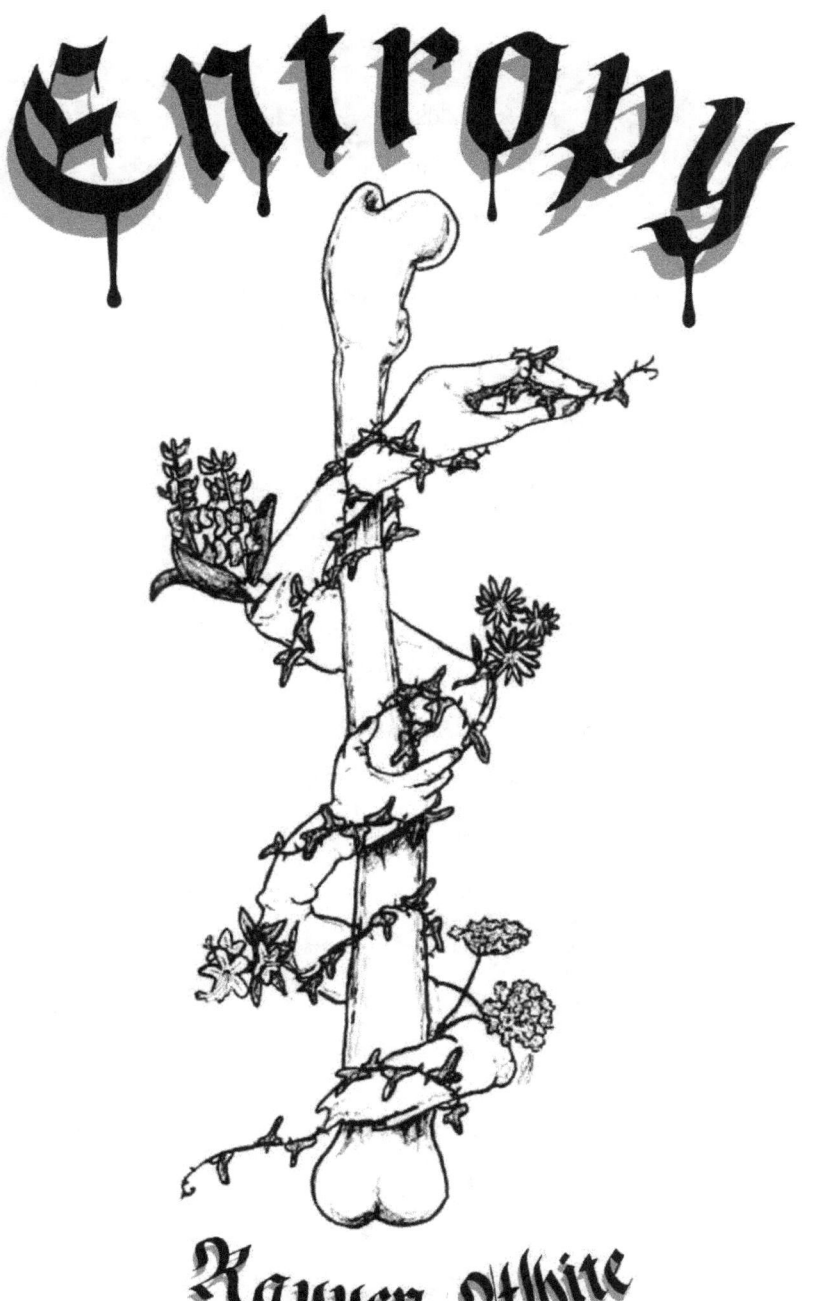

Ravven White

Cover Design by Mitch Green

Interior Illustrations by Shrike

X-ray imaging original to Ravven White

Various other illustrations licensed through Canva

No Ai was used in the writing or creation of this book.

ISBN: 978-1-959860-60-0

Printed in the United States of America

Curious Corvid Publishing, LLC
PO Box 204
Geneva, OH 44041

Curiouscorvidpublishing.com

For my daughter, Starlight

I will teach you how to make them listen and
fight for you when they still won't

Content Warnings

This book covers a variety of difficult topics from start to finish. Some of these content warnings overlap but it is my sincere wish to protect the reader. Please read with discretion.

Contains: depictions of child abuse, child neglect, mental illness/poor mental health, car accident, physical trauma, mentions of sexual assault of a minor, off page rape, painful periods, doctor neglect, various medical neglect, endometriosis, pregnancy loss, pregnancy, childbirth, hysterectomy, thoughts of suicide, multiple sclerosis

Content of Symptoms

A Referral

The thing about chronic illness is that it's *chronic,* right? It's always there. Well, at least, it's always there for *you.* The majority of people in your life, no matter how much or how little involvement they have in your day-to-day, are going to forget that. First from time-to-time, and then there will be big gaps of forgetfulness where they invite you to the beach and want you to bike across an island, forgetting that your mobility device is going to get stuck in the sand. Living with severe pain and limited mobility is exhausting as it stands, and having to remind people of your limits on a quasi-regular basis takes more energy than it is usually worth. Still, it's hard to blame them for forgetting. They're lucky that they don't have what you have—and that can be hard to reckon with, too. Resentment is a corrosive, but sometimes a little rust is the least of your problems if you're already dealing with big, sharp holes.

It's lonely, being ill. You've got a short window of time during the day where you can do anything at all, and that window is never consistent, nor is your ability. Some days you can't sit upright, and some days you can do a few dishes. If you do the dishes, you have to accept that you can't make dinner, or if you can make dinner, you definitely won't be able to write that book, knit that project, or play that video game. Those little things that make life worth living become indulgences, chores become 5k sprints, and oftentimes if you want to socialize in any moderate capacity, you have to block off an entire week—three days before to rest to make sure you're in good condition, and three days after to tenderly navigate your body, which is now the angriest at you it has ever been. And it may sound like I'm being dramatic, but I'm not. It's constant. You're always thinking about it, because your relationship with your own body has become transactional. "If I vacuum my living room, can I afford to take a shower?"

You can't afford to take a shower, and you can't afford six days of bedrest to go out to dinner and drinks with your friends (who love Uber carpools to walkable cities and uneven cobblestone sidewalks), so you stay home. Even if you live with a partner or two, you want them to go out and enjoy life as well, doing things that are not centered around you. They're the reason that the dishes stay clean and that the house hasn't gotten its own A&E reality show, after all. You get lonely, and you start to feel invisible.

That is the reason books like *Entropy* matter so much because they broadcast the words, *'I am here'*. They create a safe space to talk about your lived experiences and give others a chance to see the world through your lens. They give other disabled people a sense of community, a sense of *'I'm not alone'*. They're there to cling to when you're struggling and remind you of how far you've come. They say *'look how much I've survived'*.

Some days are bad, some days are worse, some days are pretty good. And you, the fine reader, you are here, and you are not alone.

-Sirius

PRESCRIPTION

Patient Name: ~~████~~ RAVVEN

Address: SOMETHING IS WRONG

Walk daily 30 minutes to an hour

Increase water intake

Up protein intake

Take OTC Tylenol as needed

Descent

Patient is healthy

no need for a follow up

Date: early 2000s   Signature: Doctor

Entropy

will start this the way I start everything: somewhere in the middle, way ahead of myself and still somehow behind, underprepared and overwhelmed within the first sentence. Writing anything deep and vulnerable comes at a cost and *Entropy* is no different. I sifted through poetry I had not read in years, written in the height of illness and medical neglect. I recounted old prescriptions and the harsh procedures my body had been subjected to. Some pieces drew more emotion from me than I thought they would and I would have to take a breather between them. Sometimes even between lines. I think that this is my most vulnerable and raw book I have written yet. I don't say that out of pride or as a subtle pat on the back, I say it because writing this book reminded me why I am still in therapy. It reminded me how far I have come and how far I have yet to go.

I was born a nobody in a tiny town in New York on a dark and stormy night. The first part of that is true. It's also true that October of 1990 had record breaking rain. My father had died just seven days earlier in a horrific crash. My mother told me once that she felt his presence so strongly in the delivery room that she reached out for him. He wasn't there, of course. Not physically, anyway. I was there, however, and this emptiness of father and fullness of grief seemed to set the trajectory of my life.

I'm now going to skip around a bit because *Entropy* is not about my childhood, exactly. There are other books and media for that. I will just say that I became a stepdaughter and then shortly after a stepsister and I was unloved and unwanted my

3

whole childhood. All of that is true. I was abused in just about every way you can think of, by both my mother and my stepfather, the latter inflicting increased and varied kinds of trauma as I aged. I was not listened to when I said "no". I was not listened to when I said "stop". My exhaustion and perpetually frightened demeanor were not listened to either.

This not being listened to carried over even after I got out at nineteen. I lived in a state of survival my whole stretch of twenties. I am currently thirty-four and I still live in survival, to a degree. I think I probably always will. Therapy has helped tremendously and I think everyone could benefit from it. It has helped me deconstruct my trauma, change my thinking on situations, and reclaim my mind and my body in ways I did not think possible. It is currently helping me to cope with my disabilities and navigate a life I was not ever prepared for.

Entropy is not necessarily about my childhood trauma but it does exist because of it. I would learn through my journey that my trauma and my health had become deeply intertwined. It would become nearly impossible to separate trauma response from chronic illness and symptoms. Children who endure abuse, whether it be physical or mental, carry greater percentages of life-threatening diseases, chronic pain, autoimmune disorders, and mental illness. It is hard to handle sometimes and I am often filled with painful, unanswerable questions and insurmountable grief. Do I have these things because of my genetics? Do I have these things because of the abuse and therefore would have been a healthy adult otherwise? Who is to say? These most recent days I operate on a rollercoaster of anger, grief, resentment, and radical acceptance. None of them are wrong. All of them are true.

When I was in my twenties, I started looking for answers to questions I didn't even have yet. I read books like *Childhood Disrupted* and *The Body Keeps the Score: Brain, Mind, and Body in the Healing of Trauma* which go into great detail about the lasting impacts of childhood trauma. I took the ACEs test and scored a ten and I knew my fate was sealed. Someday, at some point, it was going to catch up to me. My descent had begun.

In my early twenties, I had started going to doctors to address my painful periods and chronic back pain, both of which began occurring when I was around twelve. I think. I was told repeatedly to lose weight, drink more water, and that the pain I was experiencing was normal. When my complaints of debilitating cramps were not swayed, they put me on birth control which created more symptoms like weight gain and fatigue. My back and shoulder pain were never really addressed. It was mostly waved away as a bad period symptom. I assumed the problem had to be me. If pain was normal, maybe I was really just being a big baby. None of that was true.

I got into a relationship as twentysomethings tend to do and learned that sex was extremely painful. Not all of the time (which should have been a red flag for further examination), but enough that I was deeply insecure and never knew what to expect. I tried talking to doctors about that too but as soon as they saw a history of rape and abuse, they chalked it up to depression and anxiety and diagnosed me with vaginismus. It was just my body reliving the trauma. It had to be. Maybe it was. Or maybe, I would have learned about something called Ehlers Danlos Syndrome or Endometriosis much sooner if they had taken into account my other complaints. I tried different doctors and each one said the same. I felt like doctors were almost afraid to treat me when they saw my chart. One might think that having rape and abuse in a patient's chart would make doctors kinder, maybe more thorough, maybe more receptive to listening and believing. If any of that is true, it was not for me.

I am not saying that every doctor I ever saw was or is a bad doctor. I am sure that most of them were just doing their job as they were taught. I know there are procedures to healthcare and there are steps to diagnosis. I was just trapped on the first step for far too long and any time I thought I made progress upwards, I was sent back down again. I learned quickly that doctors didn't really see me as a whole person. I was compartmentalized into neat little boxes that never seemed to be connected. Much like the tissues in my body, this disease of unknowing and unseeing ran deep and touched everything.

The horrors I felt in my mind, my soul, my heart, and then in my body began creeping through my flesh and into the world, stealing my life away bit by bit. My body felt like a poisonous terrarium that had outgrown its vessel and broken its seal. I felt it slicing through my veins, wrapping around my ribcage, piercing through my intestines, shredding my uterus, wriggling behind my eyes, growing tendrils and blossoms through my back, threatening poison ivy on my tongue. So I did the only thing I knew how to do to contain it. I wrote.

Entropy

We aren't beginning at the beginning, we're starting somewhere in the middle*ish*. We're starting in places that I now know were the beginnings of my descent. And all of it is true.

Entropy

Growing Pains

I had horrendous growing pains as a child.
Shooting agony in hollow legs
that grew restless at bedtime.
I'd cry over them, try to rub the pains away
burning, like thistles latched onto skin.
My parents would tell me pain was normal.
("It's supposed to hurt.")
It would all go away in time.
Instead of Tylenol or doctor visits,
they stuck a bar of ivory soap under my sheets
because a radio station they listened to
every day said it was a wives' tale sure cure.
Eventually I stopped complaining.
Triumphantly, they said it worked.

We don't really ever outgrow
growing pains though, do we?
Thistles blossom to seed the next generation.
I tucked mine into bed next to me,
read them bedtime stories,
dressed them in my favorite socks
and headscarves, until one day
pain was just a part of me
and I could no longer be separated from it.

I was always nature's child.
Being outdoors was preferable to
breathing in black mold and unpredictability.
I lived under pine canopies, fascinated by
mushrooms and wildflowers,
skin perpetually stained by "grass" and "berries".

Entropy

At some point, my environment placed its claim.

Spores. Seeds. Roots.

While I was at my bedroom window
counting constellations with stars in my eyes,
my body was seeding pains that would last a lifetime.
How was I to know, kicking soap in my sheets?
Would I have added an extra bar?
Would I have tucked them all in next to me?
Would I have chopped up extra mushrooms
and boysenberries into my wildwood soup?

Perhaps this poem doesn't make sense but
neither did my childhood
neither did the soap in my sheets
neither did the growing pains—well except

those make sense to me now because

They called it growing pains but

Now I call it Ehlers Danlos Syndrome, Complex PTSD,
Multiple Sclerosis, Endometriosis, Grief and Loss and
Trauma...

We never really outgrow growing pains, do we?

Somewhere out there beneath pines and stars,
a ghost of me is chopping mushrooms and
crushing boysenberries into wildwood soup
wondering if magic is real and if I will ever feel safe.

I want to tell her yes.

What Did You Do on Summer Vacation?

I didn't see the car when it hit us.
I was in the passenger seat,
daydreaming as twelve-year-olds do.
The impact
A
R
R
I
V
E
D
Metal on metal
G a s p i n g
B u r n i n g

My mother kept asking if I was okay.
I think I answered.
I must have said something—
                    something hurts, my neck, my neck—
"SOMEBODY CALL 911!"
Ambulance.
Lights.
They strapped me down, collared me,
asked me my name.
I think I answered.
I must have said something—
                    my neck—my shoulder—my arm?!
I remember everything was silent.
Everything was loud.
My heart was racing
r a c i n g

I couldn't breathe,
        I couldn't breathe

       icouldntbreatheicouldntbreatheicouldnt—
BUMP

They unloaded me,
wished me healing and a
happy summer vacation
because I was twelve and
they assumed I was happy.
Maybe I was.
        I must have said I was.

After that, my memory is foggy.
I can't quite recall a diagnosis
or even a direction.
Only hushed conversations
But I can recall the doctor warning me:
      "You'll be in a lot of pain.
      Try to be still."
And there was pain, a lot of it.
It ached into the core of me,
radiated from my neck to my fingertips
and nothing helped it.
      "It's supposed to hurt.
      Try to be still."
I remember my younger sibling crying.
      They cried all of the time.
I told my mother to lay him on me
so she could sleep.

12

Entropy

I, a baby, held a baby
swaddled in pain and unheard cries.
I learned how to hold it in.

I still blame myself sometimes,
that if I hadn't learned
so early on

> *"It's supposed to hurt.*
> *Try to be quiet."*

maybe someone would have
listened to me sooner.

Entropy

Germination

And I wonder how long it will take
before these bruises in my bones
transpose as time and weather
instead of this brutal imprint—
the sowing of his hands on me.

Entropy

𝔓𝔯𝔬𝔳𝔢𝔯𝔟𝔰 31

When I was younger my strength was my pride.
I could toss a fifty-pound bag of bird feed
across unscarred shoulders,
tread it into our rotting barn.
~~My parents~~ *They* praised me for it,
for being the *right kind* of strong feminine.
I swallowed labored breaths,
not knowing I was also swallowing spores
that would take root in muscles,
make a home for themselves
in the one thing I thought I could hold onto.
Meanwhile, I would cradle two babies,
one on each hip, in each arm.
I was not their mother but
they reached for me like one
and I loved them like one.
I would spend hours on hours
cleaning and scrubbing *Their* home,
cooking for hungry, wanting mouths.
Days disappeared in mounds of
dirty laundry, crusty dishes,
molding walls decorated in
crayon portraits hiding holes.
I never tired.
I never faltered.
I was fifteen and my strength was my pride.
Strong legs, strong back.
Unmovable.
Unbreakable.
Unlovable.

Entropy

It didn't matter if I ached,
it was the body getting stronger.
Pain was part of the process.
Pain was expected.
Pain was demanded.
~~("It's supposed to hurt.")~~

I learned not to cry—
not over torn muscles
not over finger imprinted hips
not over cracked hands
dried and bleeding.
Strength was my pride.
Strength was how I endured.
Now I am thirty-four and
much of my strength is gone.
I could not lift bird feed
or carry babies in any capacity,
neither in arms or ovaries or womb.
The things I cradle now are
far heavier and far more painful.
The spores I inhaled in my youth
settled into me, spread over me.
A sleeping sickness waiting silently
each time he penetrated me,
when he broke both my hymen
and my skin, mapped me in bruises
that left invisible scars that will never heal.
My body creaks and snaps and groans
a protest to being too strong too soon
and for far, far too long.
I do cry now, oceans of tears.
I cry over worn-out muscles
and disintegrating bones,

18

and a cracked heart—
irregular and abused.
Have I grown weaker?
The left side of my body struggles,
my hand shaking, as I stare at it
begging it to do what I ask.
"I miss being strong," I tell myself
gazing in the mirror, raking
over a body that is no longer fifteen,
no longer strong—at least
not the way it had to be.
It was strong enough to live
through the unworthy *Them.*

Will it now be strong enough
to live for me?
Is there enough of me left?
Tears stream and
I do not stop them.

Entropy

Here I Am, Locked Inside Again . . .

Don't leave me alone in the quiet!
For a long time, all that I had was silence
locked in a cage created for violence.
It was a triumph if someone remembered me,
to let me out if I had to pee
or needed a drink or needed to feed.
Hours and hours in solitary confinement
with bruises bestowed each day for refinement—
beat the devil out of me.
Beat the sinfulness out of me.
Beat me until my skin resembles your own kind of sin
so maybe you can forget what you did.
Best to begin when I'm sleeping.
Dissociate so that I might keep breathing.
I can't tell you the fear of a locked room,
don't leave me here, don't shut me in.
Fists beating walls that won't ever cave in.
Days turn to months as the seasons change
and my hopes rearrange as my birthday came.
But it was just another casualty
regretting the existence of me.
I swallowed my voice in the violence
and I sat alone in the silence.
I sat alone in the darkness
and nobody heard me crying.

Don't leave me alone in the quiet...

Entropy

Dysesthesia

(Sometimes I
want to die)
Watch pieces of me
d
  i
    s
      i
        n
          t
            e
              g
                r
                  a
                    t
                      e
              into ~~nothingness~~
like an old
picture or
a memory you
can't quite
recall...
(Sometimes I
want to die)
        Sometimes I
           am ~~nothing~~
             at all.

Entropy

My mother made me

pulled me from her womb

titanium bones and supple flesh

a soft heart

"a soft heart"

I repeat this to remind myself

as my mother, my bones, and my flesh

have all failed me

who shall I become now?

Entropy

Leo

If you were to hide an object
behind a piece of paper,
and place the paper on a mirror,
the mirror can still show you
the paper's secrets
thanks to the infinite rays
of light and refraction,
of energy traveling so fast
to deliver us messages,
to give us our reflections.

If you were to hide an object
behind a piece of paper
and show me the paper,
I would very likely not
be able to see and know what is on
the other side.
Try as I might to be reflective,
try as I might to be light,
my energy is s l o w .
My transformative realization takes
t i m e .

I often feel that my final self is the mirror,
my present is the paper,
the object the future,
and my past the clearest,
most definitive reflection that I can see.
But if I place myself in between,
and view my body, my heart, my worth
as a reflection of both past and future,

Entropy

I see the reflections of the past:
Brokenness. Failure. Heartache. Disease.
But also:
Persistence. Resilience.
And in the present I see something
the past didn't have:
Healing. Wellness. Peace. Acceptance.

If I am energy passing between two places,
I marvel at the one I am becoming,
and I have to trust that whatever is
reflecting back at me,
whatever is behind the paper
is worth living for.

PRESCRIPTION

Patient Name: ~~XXXXX~~ RAVVEN

Address: ArE YOU LiStEniNG

Mono-linyah 28 tablet

Take 1 tablet by mouth once a day

OTC Midol for cramps as needed

Walk daily

Increase water intake

Decline

Referred patient to
nutrition specialist
Recommended therapy

Date: 2010s   Signature: Doctor

Entropy

The only memory I have of my twenties when it comes to my health or my body is that of discomfort, pain, and the anxiety of not knowing when it was going to fall apart. I can hear the echoes of older generations thundering down to remind me that I was too young for any of that. I was too young to be sick. I was too young to be in pain. I was too young to be anxious about falling apart. All of that is false.

After a harrowing escape from a childhood home that had done its best to extinguish me, I was doing everything I could to keep my very fragile light alive. I lived in a high-security battered women's shelter for a while waiting for my story to make it to court, only for a plea deal to be arranged and accepted, a bitter end to my (lack of) justice that I am still not over. While living at home with equally traumatized siblings and an abusive mother, battling extremely dangerous mental health issues alone, I got a job and started college. I attempted to immerse myself into a world I knew nothing about which did not have time for a homeschooled, backwoods, ex-cult conservative girl. The drip of cortisol that began in my childhood continued. My survival was far from over.

In these tumultuous times, my period was coming and going according to its own purpose. I never knew when to expect it. Sometimes it would come every 28 days and other times not show up for three to six months. When it did finally come, I would bleed so profusely and cramp so painfully I thought surely I was going to die. Sometimes I would lock myself into a college toilet and bleed into it and wonder how long it would take before anyone realized I was even missing. I did not care enough for myself to want to stay. By this time, I had started making other friends and had joined a women's support group through the shelter I had been in. Hard and painful periods were normal, I was told. All women suffered. I had suffered since I was at least twelve, probably younger, in hindsight. I was no stranger to pain. I was no stranger to enduring. I had kept painful, shameful secrets locked inside me for decades. One more was nothing.

Besides being chronically ill, I was also chronically poor. On days when the period came and I couldn't afford pads or didn't have them on hand, I wadded up the toilet paper and prayed. I started wondering to who, exactly. What benevolent, all-knowing God would allow all of this suffering? I had no answer but I prayed anyway. When the bleeding started unexpectedly, I would excuse myself from class in a panic, feeling the blood and tissue dribble down my leg on days the periods caught me in skirts. I'd try not to faint from not having eaten that day and convince myself that a Snickers bar from the vending machine was good enough because it had peanuts for my brain and surely that was fuel enough.

I remember thinking so unkindly of my body during this time, that I was chubby in all the wrong places, hiding in long skirts and oversized sweaters. I have no idea what size I wore or how much I weighed, and it doesn't matter because that version of my body was trying so hard to keep me alive. It deserved so much better than I had been able to give. We both did.

I started getting pains in my right side when I was around twenty-two. The nausea would come in waves so bad I wouldn't be able to eat for days. I would get fevers and chills and stabbing pain that would double me over so bad I couldn't walk. After an episode put me in the ER I learned I had gallbladder disease and stones, and I would need to have the organ removed. Not right away but soon. The doctor on duty told me to stop abusing my body with an unhealthy diet and to eat better and drink more water. I remember wondering if he knew what it was like to be excited for blood drives because they gave you chipotle gift cards in exchange for donating your blood and it meant I got to eat for free instead of choosing between filling my gas tank or my stomach. Or if he knew that the one free meal I got at work every day courtesy of McDonald's meant I also got to eat that day.

Over the next year the attacks continued to get worse until one finally landed me in the hospital. I had an infection that had become threatening. My gallbladder was shooting bile back into my system and it was only a matter of time before I would go septic. This doctor was compassionate. He was worried. He begged me to stay and have the surgery.

"I can do it today," he told me. *"This can all be over today. I can make your pain stop."*

But I couldn't afford the surgery, let alone the hospital stay. I pulled my body out of the bed and dragged myself home. I had to go back to work. Medicaid still wouldn't approve the surgery for me, working at minimum wage and going to college. I had to keep on toughing it out. So I did. I worked. I saved. I got sicker. I hoped I didn't die.

My home life only added to the stress and anxiety. I will never claim to be a perfect person. I will claim that the twenty-two-year-old version of me desperately tried to be. I wanted my mom to love me and be proud of me, but it seemed like nothing I did would achieve that. We were constantly fighting: my mother berating me at every opportunity and me screaming defensively back until I learned to just shut up and take it. Much as I had before. I was also trapped in an abusive relationship which seemed like the only way to get out of the living situation with my mom. For a while I lived out of my car when I could because it was better than being at home. I showered at school. I cleaned cars for spare change. I survived. All of this is true.

Eventually I realized I was being cheated on and I got out of the bad relationship. I met someone else who is now my current partner. I moved away from my mom and thought it would help our relationship. I continued working. I kept my grades up at school. I kept hoping I would someday have a normal family.

Eventually I ended up back in the ER, this time with a different doctor who told me that my time for waiting was over. He explained to me the hospital would work with me on a payment plan for the surgery. All I needed was one thousand dollars as a downpayment for the surgery. As usual, I went back to work. I cut my classes to save on travel and trimmed back on expenses as much as possible. I was a chronically ill person struggling in a world that did not have time for me. This is true. However, I was also a chronically ill person who had people who genuinely cared.

A very kind coworker whom I will never forget gifted me the final portion of money I needed for my downpayment. She tried to be sneaky about it, putting it in a green notebook and handing it to the manager on duty who then handed it to me. Inside was the money alongside some American Reject lyrics that I can't include because of copyright reasons. But let's just say all I could do was be strong and keep on moving. I will never forget her or that kindness and I hope someday to be able to do something that extraordinary for someone else. And if you happen to read this, I'm putting something here just for you that only you will understand:

Hawkeye's butt.

I called my doctor the next day and scheduled my surgery. My current partner stayed by my side through the whole thing. On the day of surgery when I opened my eyes, he was there holding my hand. I asked for my mom, but she had left before I had even woke up.

I learned to adjust for a lack of a gallbladder. Several years down the line I learned to adjust for a lack of a mother. Sometimes I still have phantom pains.

All of that is true.

Entropy

Fertilizer

I'm struggling under the weight
of expectation, chained by limitation,
trying to find a way to make it,
hoping someone will understand it—
what is wrong with me?

This moment won't be forever,
but it is my forever, for now.

Entropy

Entropy

Referral to Psychology

If I am pretty,
will the doctor hear me?
Or will he breeze right past me
another pretty face without bones?

If I am ugly,
will the doctor hear me?
Or will he shudder silently
and hurriedly send me home?

If I am crying,
will the doctor hear me?
Or will he just label me
as an anxiety ridden fiend?

If I am vocal
will the doctor hear me?
Or will compassion dissolve completely
and dismiss knowledge I have gleaned?

If I am...but...I *am*.
And the doctor *should* hear me
as I languish in my agony
suffering in body, not in head.

destructive diagnoses lead to death

Entropy

Is It A Symptom or Hallucination?

I close my eyes and drift into an uneasy sleep.
Images dance in random sequence
how many secrets that you keep
Forgetful fingers drumming weakness
eyes open, but not awake, not living
eyes closed, blinking through static hollows
what is it that follows, breathing
Rage fueled lungs relax into shallow.
In this phantasmagoria of unending daydream,
If I am awake, am I living? If not, am I dead?
are you lucid while you're dreaming
Lost in a labyrinth birthed from your head.
Dreaming? Sleeping? Wide awake?
My days are numbered, so who's to say?

Entropy

Who Will Believe Me?

I woke from a slumber I could not remember
eyes opened as if I had just closed them
I would not say that I suffered, simply slumbered.
I try to recall my name, slipping down the drain
just barely caressing a forgotten remembering
I smile contentedly, understanding I have met the end of me.

Entropy

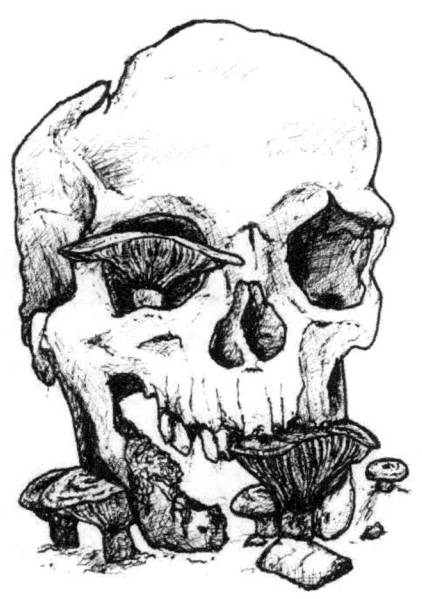

Do I Believe Me?

And if you knew her
you would not know her,
as consuming darkness
multiplies within her.

Entropy

Dystonia

Sometimes I am too tired
to even write poetry.
The words are there but
              they remain trapped
              a muscle reflex
              pained and distended.
I grasp at them desperately,
massage, drug, force flex.
Sometimes it relents but
              I remain trapped
              a muscle reflex
              captive to myself.

Entropy

Gethsemane

I know it seems silly
but as I lay pinned beneath agony
I prayed one last time.
I begged for intervention—
divine salvation—
from the crushing weight
grinding holes into hips
that was surely here to
swallow me,
digest me,
spit me out and bury me
for the final time.
My god, my god, why have you forsaken me?
When I opened my eyes,
the only hands clinging to the bed were mine
and I remembered I am alone.

Entropy

Cymbalta, 90mg

I am depressed.
I offer you thornless roses
as I swallow bitter spores
behind my unlined petal lips,
midnight colors bleeding into skin.
My forced smile comes naturally to me,
a trellis of traumas stitched into place.

I am depressed.
The Shadows in my closet
and under my bed fear of me.
They tremble at the mutterings in sleep
because no monster is as scary
as the one we call 'friend'.
The spirit world doesn't stand a chance
in the face of deep seated *mycelium* memories.

I am depressed.
My bed evolves to my rooted coffin,
a plethora of flora and fauna
springing from the rot of my collapse.
I imagine the blue gills of the *lactarius indigo*
will match my budding veins.
I reason that it's not poison
and neither am I. *Am I?*

I am depressed.
Limb by limb my body folds in on me,
weak and heavy, lifeless,
spine contorting in misery,

51

arms bent at odd angles beneath me
but I will not move, cannot move.
Pain is not even enough to drive me.
I decompose bitterly.

I am depressed.
It is no longer enough to offer help.
It is no longer enough to offer care.
Further and further I crumble
blending with the damp graveyard dirt
that I did not even dig myself.
Spongey roots of regret and repentance
take hold and imprison me.

I am depressed.
I stir in my bed of indigo mushrooms.
They are beginning to die
and I begin to learn what letting go
actually looks like.
When I move, the snaps and crackles
astound and amaze me
I didn't know I had this power within me,
a resurrected body unfolding.

I am depressed.
Warm showers fall on bruised skin,
tired eyes, scarred thighs.
I water the dirt collecting at my feet.
and pot a mushroom with its flowers
because I know this sorrow
will never truly be gone.
All I can do is manage it.

Entropy

I am depressed.
It's been days—weeks?—
Since I spoke.
My vocal cords wheeze as I
say *"goodbye"* and *"no"* and *"I'm not ready"*.
I didn't even know it had that vocabulary.
I'm sorry mother, but you brought me
spores and sorrows and damp grave dirt.

I am depressed.
My smile is less stitches more ivy,
a trellis spotted in indigo against midnight.
It almost looks like a velvet night sky.
I am mindful of my flora and fauna
mindful of the spores people place in my lungs.
My bed, my coffin, comforts me
but does not contain me.

I am depressed.
Wherever I go there will be traces of bruises
framed in wistful, twisted ivy.
Feet that seem to never shake
this damp graveyard dirt.
I have learned that my mushrooms
Need not be poisonous
thus neither shall I be.

I am depressed
but I am learning what it truly means
to let go, what it means to
sow my sorrows into gardens.
There will always be indigo spores
lingering in my decomposition
but they will not be the only thing that grows.

53

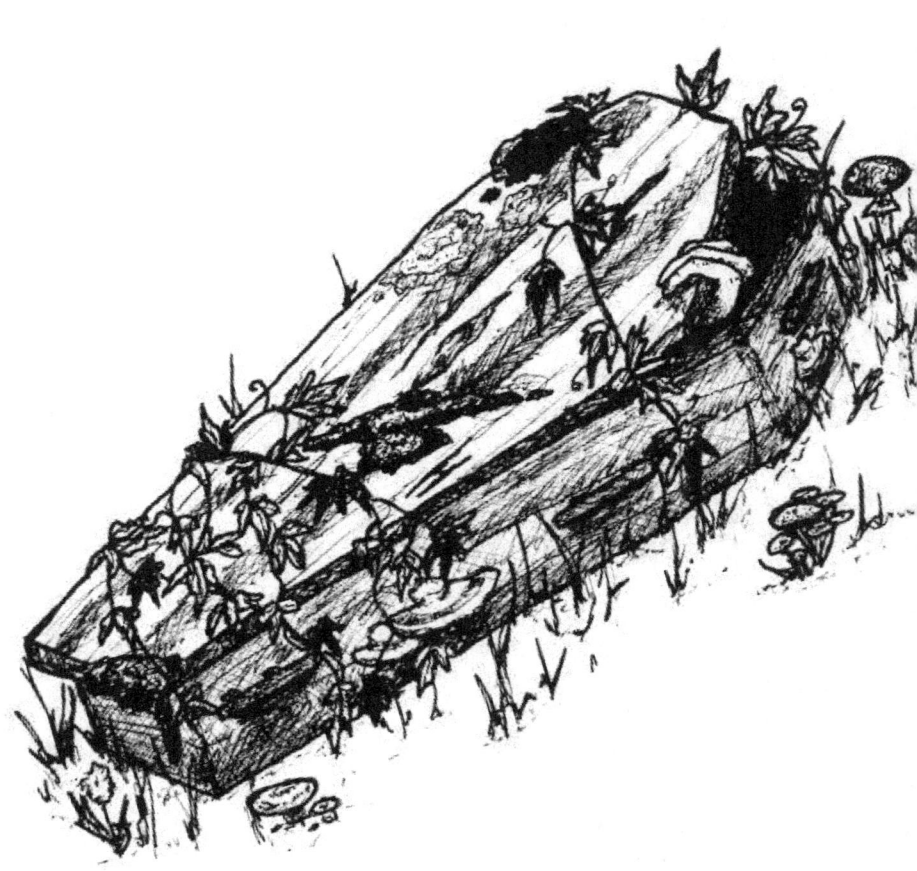

They Put Stars in My Eyes

He compared me to a Botticelli
and it broke me—
I have never viewed this body as art,
rather, an unfinished canvas—
smudged, blurry, too ill defined
to be anything besides a "if only".
Perhaps I just needed a painter,
fingers softly tracing features,
who could reverently
bring my artwork into focus.

Entropy

Autophobia Syndrome

When I finally break,
will you be there?
Will you puzzle me
together? Soft edges,
worn corners with faded borders?
Or will I shatter into
millions of fractures...
                    Stardust?
So delicate all you can do
is watch me dance through
your puzzled fingers.
Will I drift into the cosmos,
or fade into nothingness?
I am too tired to piece myself together,
brittle glue and faded tape.
Just let me
            b r e a k .

Entropy

58

Self-Titled Album

Some days I am more statue than human
Please, please do not touch me.
I will crumble beneath your kindness,
disintegrate to your violence.
I sit quietly, creeping vines suffocating joints.
I am locked in place as it overtakes me,
tiny tendrils extending to fingertips.
I am so full I fear it will burst out of me—
fire burning blossoms blooming in eye sockets,
bitter three-leaf foliage coating my tongue.
Let the blood pour from penetrated eardrums,
replace it with gushing water and nutrients,
force my faulty circulation to sustain itself.
They will find me, a bust of bones, overgrown.
I sit quietly, dissociating into illusion.
Some days I am more statue than human,
waiting for the entropy to consume me.

Entropy

High White Blood Cells, Abnormally Low Vit. D

It is morning and I am on fire again.
He tries to douse it with Tylenol and coffee,
ibuprofen and arthritis cream,
help me limp to the shower where
cascades of cleansing dilute me.
Nothing can reach the fires though.
It leaks out of my eyes,
evaporates the cold sweat on my skin.
I am being burned alive on the inside by
a body that doesn't understand
I. Am. Not. The. Enemy.
It follows the fuel of facets, traveling my spine
lodging in my neck, extending to shoulders
and elbows and wrists and fingers.
Pathing down choked nerves so deeply
that sometimes I am not sure I still have toes.
I wait to fall to ruin, charred bits of bones
strung together by poison ivy and flint.
Perhaps they will put me on medical display
*"Behold this body, rotted from the inside,
twisted tendrils and mycelium muscles."*
The fires burn endlessly, a constant cycle
of degenerative growth, decay, rebirth.
I sigh, exhaling smoke and spores,
counting down the minutes to more Tylenol,
more creams, and a dousing that will not work.

Entropy

Familial Distortion

I spent over an hour explaining myself to you:
why these bruises linger on my skin,
why my hands fall to the side, limp,
the heaviness of my existence
speaking through tremors and palpitations
I have no need of angel tongue.
This is not Divinity, it is not holy,
I am foreign to healthy
though I seek asylum in you.
You said, *"I still believe you will become better."*
And that's when I realized your true horror:
I'm still alive.
You can't, *won't*, see it eating me inside.
It is too monstrous to imagine
that young and beautiful
has become corrupted and vengeful.
I'm still alive.

Of course I will thrive.

Entropy

Symptoms I Can't Say Out Loud

Life screams virtuously at me:
"You are not worth much
if you are not working!"
I lie heaving, burning, twisting, aching.
I am slowly disintegrating,
a skeleton gnawed by degeneration
and generational entropy.
"I am not worth anything,
I am not worth saving."
I weep bitterly and
self-medicate accordingly.

Entropy

This Did Not Make Me Stronger

"I don't have the option to lay in bed!"
What do you think I do all day?
If this was your Last Supper
would I be at the center?
Or do you see me as Judas—
betrayed by a kiss
and a misdiagnosis?
This is my cross to bear,
not yours, not his, not hers.
Eat away holes in my wrists,
I didn't ask for any of this!
I will bear it,
I will break under it.
Are these your silver coins or mine?

Entropy

"No One Is Stronger Than You, Mommy!"

I cry for my daughter,
lamenting this world
I have brought her into.
Will she be thought of
as more than soft flesh?
There is no protection
from the brutal separation
of lips—grown, I am still
a burial for callous stakes
I cannot escape.
How will I teach her to speak
when I cannot hold myself
together?

Entropy

I Can Never Go Home

I would like to visit you but
your plot of land by the river
underneath the trees is too far from me:
a stone's throw amongst headstones,
a gaping cavern from my
plot of land by the sea, underneath the stars.
I would like to visit you,
bring trinkets and photographs,
drink sweet tea and crunch pickles,
7 Up poured into overflowing cups
and I'll joke about bringing guacamole
which I know you hate...d.
I would like to visit you,
to sink into the mossy grave beside you
and perhaps, for a moment,
know what your embrace felt like.
Perhaps if our bones decayed together,
my phoenix ash could transmute your dust
and maybe, just maybe,
I could feel something besides grief,
which is all I have known you as.
I would like to visit you,
alone, unencumbered. Nightfall.
Tell you all the things I withhold,
fragile pieces of an ancient soul
slowly crumbling.
I wish I could visit you,
so I light candles and say prayers.
I prop your photo on my table,
surround it with candy and pickles
and cups overflowing with 7 Up
which my child sneakily drinks from—

and for a moment, just a moment,
I swear I hear the ringing laughter
of a voice I never go to know.
I wish I could visit you,
but you visit me, all the time,
don't you?
Death is not the end, not really,
and truly your grave is surely empty.
Oh grave where is thy victory?
Oh death where is thy sting?
I would like to visit you,
see the tomb they placed you in,
but I know you are not really there.
It's the ringing laughter
that tells me you visit me, here.

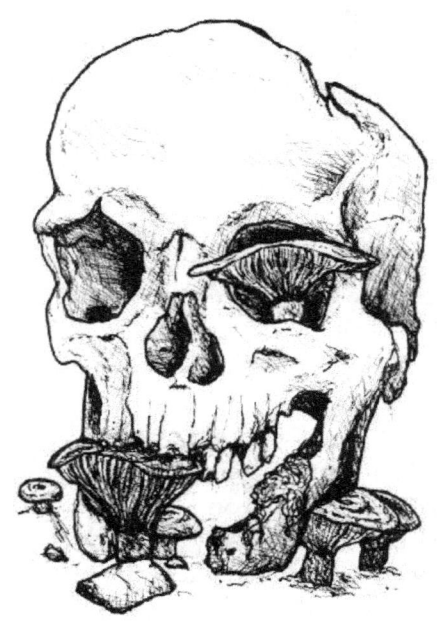

Chronic Fantasies

And someday when I'm
finally done writing sad poetry
maybe that will be enough

When the last blood is bled
and my pen falls, uninterrupted
to an eternal slumber,

maybe that will be enough.
Each time I promise myself
that this sad one will be
the last sad one,

Oh how easily I lie to myself.

Sun dances on a forgotten tomb
and I rise not on the third day
not even on the sixth day,
but the forgotten one.

Someday when it is all over
maybe it will be enough
and I will no longer rise,
forgotten,
and I will no longer write sad poetry.

Entropy

To Be Loved Is to Be Seen

My husband calls me an emotional powerhouse.
"I have never seen you meek," he says.
"Even when I am weak?" I reply.
"I have never seen you weak.
I have seen you sad, seen the bottomless
depth of a heart left for rot
but I have absolutely not
ever seen you weak.
There is power in your sadness
just as much as there is power in your gladness
and no one can ever take that from you."
I call him a fool,
rivulets cascading from a powerhouse
overflowing.

Entropy

Some Scars Are Decorations

Around the house, I let my skin breathe
adorned in crop tops and velvet.
I dance in the kitchen listening to Glass Animals.
My body moves, unprohibited by
choking buttons and pinching zippers,
smooth jeans that outline flawless curves
hiding the home my children created.
Sewn into padded bras with extra lifts,
high waisted pants stitched twice at the hip,
my hands trace an outline that is merely illusion
as my body suffocates for perfection.
In the sanctity of my home, I breathe,
allowing my body the space it deserves,
desires, the space that ought to be admired;
Oh, how little I have loved myself.
Vulnerability clashes within me
watching my daughter trace spots on my body
as though they were constellations, not scars
as though they were swirling lights on an inky night—
sepia stained maps that have seen wreckage
that somehow still leads to unfathomable treasure.
She traces stretch marks along my side
paving the way to a soft stomach where she lays her head.
"Boo boo, mommy?" She whispers.
My partner follows the path she traced,
stretch marks splotched with freckles meeting on a jagged scar.
"Leftover decorations from when you lived there," he replies.
She hugs me and her hands brush raised lines on my shoulders,
a soft touch on violent self-hurt decades old.
She does not understand as I cry.
"Boo boo, mommy?"

"Old ones. They are better now.
They just mean I'm alive."
I touch them thoughtfully, as I trace hands on this body,
this body built specifically for me.
I bare my skin, scars and all,
as I look at the stranger in the mirror.
Oh, how little I have loved myself.
Oh, how little.
So I bare myself in my home,
get to know the stranger in the mirror.
I dance to Glass Animals in crop tops and velvet
so that my daughter will know that the constellations she traces
holds the beauty of galaxies not fully understood.

Bend. Don't Break.

When you live with chronic pain
sometimes you are forced to sit and wait
and those of us who must sit and wait
can sometimes hear and see the things others cannot.
Today it took me longer to get out of my car
and I sat with the door open
counting the heartbeats it took me to breathe
and I watched the trees swaying in the wind
and I heard them creak.
I watched the top of the canopy
bending to a force beyond its control,
leaning and twisting
but never breaking.
It was comforting to see
I was not the only one withstanding.
I was not the only one bending
I was not the only one creaking.
And, much like the trees,
I would not be found breaking.
Today I was reminded
of the beauty found in nature
and if nature can run parallels
with trees, roots anchored deep
still bending and heaving
not breaking
not breaking
not breaking–

Maybe I will make it, too.

Entropy

PRESCRIPTION

Patient Name: ~~███~~ **RAVVEN**

Address: nothing is Working

Folic Acid 1MG by mouth once daily
Medroxyprogesterone 10 mg once daily
from day 15 to day 24 at menstrual cycle
Metformin HGL 350 MG Twice daily
Ondansetron ODT 8MG 1 under the tongue
3x a day as needed for nausea

Delay

No refills
Patient referred to infertility counseling
Referred to weight loss clinic

Date: 2018   Signature: Doctor

Entropy

was raised with the belief that the most valuable part of my being was my womb and that my ability to create and sustain life was my greatest purpose. My truest happiness would come from the number of babies I would produce. I read Bible verses of women who did not "bear fruit" or who had difficulty conceiving children and how they were cursed, cast aside, and meant to endure terrible tragedies in the hopes of one day carrying to term. Children were a gift, I was a vessel, and if I could not carry, I was defective, disappointing, *pointless*. None of that was true.

This kind of teaching lingers. It poisons your thinking, leeches into the marrow of you. Of course children are a gift, but they are not the only gift a person can create. Besides possessing a womb, I possessed a brain. I was incredibly smart, one of those gifted people that could easily pick up just about anything new and learn it without a problem. I was curious, invested, and I questioned everything. My options were limitless—or at least, they could have been. Perhaps if I had been found sooner, if I had gotten therapy sooner, if I had received some kind of intervention sooner…I digress.

The point is, eventually the time came that I did want children. With that want came the poison that I had been taught about my true calling and my true purpose. It made what was to come far more cruel than it should have been.

The first time I was pregnant, I didn't realize right away. My partner and I had just been married a year, had just gotten the keys to our first house. At the time I was on the pill, but we had been talking about when we might want to start trying and I had been a little lazy on the dosage timing every day. We were still being careful though, or at least we thought we were. I remember feeling more tired than usual, but I attributed that to moving. I was never a good tracker and since my periods were inconsistent, I didn't think anything of it when it didn't come.

And then it did. But it was different.

I had nausea and stomach cramps so deep and so painful I thought that my insides were coming out of me. In the toilet were blood and clumps of tissues that looked different—it felt different. At the time the only doctor I could afford to go to and see was Planned Parenthood and the closest one to me was an hour away. I called them on the phone and told them what was happening and what I was experiencing. They told me it was likely a miscarriage and told me to take a pregnancy test. I did so, with trembling hands. The pink line emerged. They urged me to go to the ER. I hung up.

I was in shock.

I did not go to the ER.

I could not face this loss that I hadn't even known existed. I bled and cried and vomited and sweated and I tried not to think about the women in the Bible.

I looked for a baby. There wasn't one, of course. It had to have been very early, too early for anything beyond clumps of tissues and the most gut-wrenching pain I had ever experienced in my life.

I went through it alone. I did not tell my partner, feigning it as a bad period. I buried this child into me. I was too afraid.

Even though I was years and years removed from the things I'd been taught and even though I didn't believe them anymore, our society is still so heavily rooted in the identity of what makes a woman a woman. Her womb, her fertility, her creation tied to children. And then we pity the women who opt not to have children, how will she find fulfillment? Who will take care of her when she is older? Who will perpetuate the cycle that we have structured our lives in?

Eventually I healed, I moved on, and I planted little flowers on the grave in my heart, and I invited my partner to do the same. A few years later, we decided to try again, this time on purpose and with intention. It was time to start our family.

I was terrified.

We took our vitamins, I tracked my period and ovulation cycle, and we had the proper scheduled sex to make sure we hit our peak times. We did everything we were supposed to do. Link would go to the store and pick up the early detection pregnancy tests and I would take them, not too early but definitely on time.

And every single one was negative.

We tried for about three months on our own before we saw the first doctor. She evaluated me, ran some tests, told me to lose weight and drink more water. We returned to our regularly scheduled programming; I started walking and drinking more water. I wasn't losing weight even though I was trying. We were active and on schedule. I upped my vitamins and started researching which diets would help fertility.

The tests remained negative.

Three months later we went back to the doctor. She diagnosed me with Polycystic Ovarian Syndrome (PCOS) after more blood tests and after an ultrasound we discovered cysts on my ovaries which accounted for some of the terrible pain I experienced during my cycle. She theorized that my ovaries weren't sending eggs out the way they were supposed to which was reducing our fertility even more. She brought up my weight again and I said that I was trying but I just wasn't having any luck losing on my own. She decided to put me on metformin to bring it down some as well as restarting birth control in order to jumpstart my cycle and hopefully reset my system.

I remember feeling so distraught and defeated during this time. Like I was going backwards by going back on birth control. The dose they gave me was higher. It made me feel sick and so did the metformin. It tore up my stomach and made me nauseous all the time. I was miserable. I cried much of the time. I didn't understand why my body didn't want to do what it was supposed to be made to do. Why was I defective? Had I missed out on the one opportunity I'd had?

Eventually the birth control worked and my period did come. However, the birth control also caused me to gain more weight thanks to the high estrogen (this would be interesting to know later when I was finally diagnosed with endometriosis and adenomyosis). The doctor blamed the weight gain on me instead.

We were now approaching almost a full year of infertility the last time we went to see this doctor. She sat us down and very bluntly said:

"You will never have children. You had one miscarriage before, and you haven't had a positive test since and your periods are too unpredictable now. You are too poor to afford in vitro. So, I am giving it to you straight: You are not going to have children. You can keep trying on your own but there is nothing more I can do for you."

Link held my hand and I sobbed quietly and never felt more defective in my whole life.

We asked more questions, but nobody could really tell us *why*. There were no definitive answers to my fertility, just generalized *"there seems to be a lot going on"*. Looking back now, I wish I had demanded better care, more answers, more something. But the bitter truth is, the doctor was right: we were poor. We couldn't afford health insurance, and we were paying for everything out of pocket. In her mind, I think she was trying to spare us.

Did you know that on average for any illness it takes four doctors and $50,000 to get a diagnosis? And that is *just* a diagnosis. After that comes the care, the procedures, the medicine, and who knows what else.

For a long time, I thought of this doctor through a lens of cruelty and disinterest. I think of her now through a lens of reality and crushing compassion and I wonder if she saw my reality clearer than I was capable of in that moment.

I held a lot of anger in me during this time. It burned me up. I resented the societal expectation that I *needed* to have children based on the commentary I faced on daily basis at work. By this time, I was working alongside my partner at his family's business and one thing about family businesses is that the customers can get a little too familiar. They get to know you and your family and the things that are happening and pretty soon, they think they are somehow an extended part of your family too. They start offering unwelcomed and unwanted attentions, thoughts, and opinions. I was told everything from the fact that I owed my in-laws grandchildren (something my in-laws had never thought or expressed), to how many children I should have and when, to how I should deliver my children. I even had a woman in the middle of a rush hour stand next to me while I was checking out customers and explain in graphic detail how to focus on my vagina during childbirth so I didn't need any pain medication! The comments were relentless and took a toll on my mental health. What started out as me feeling like a failure to my family turned into feeling like a failure to my community and I couldn't take the idea of whispers and averted glances and, god forbid, suggestions when they found out I was infertile. I kept my smile, cried in the backroom at work and at home on the weekends. People around me told me to keep the faith, gave me unsolicited fertility advice, pitiful glances, and continued to ask the awful, ignorant question:

"When are you going to start having children?"

Meanwhile, in quiet hours, I wrote poetry longing for a baby I only ever dreamed about. You will read a lot of this poetry ahead. Much of it I chose not to heavily edit because I wanted to leave it as I wrote it. I wanted the emotion to stay as it was. I did want a child. I wanted the chance to be a mother, a parent, and a good one. I felt I could be a good one. But I wanted to be okay with not having one and the circumstances around me made me feel like it was wrong of me to want that.

I held out hope for a little while. I took more pink tests. And then the fall came and the trees gave in to their seasonal little deaths, and I decided maybe it was my turn as well.

I gave up. I let go. I accepted that it was over.

At the end of September in 2018 I started feeling terribly sick. I was weak, nauseous, my body ached all the time, my breasts hurt terribly, and I was met with a constant, debilitating fatigue. As it happened, I had made an appointment with a different gynecologist to investigate my painful periods more, the word *endometriosis* appearing for the first time as a possible cause for my infertility and debilitating cramps.

On October 2nd, 2018, I saw my brand new doctor and ran through all my symptoms and she offered a new treatment plan including exploratory surgery to look for endometrium lesions. At the very end of the appointment, she asked me to pee in a cup for a pregnancy test, *just in case*. I laughed in her face. I peed in the cup anyway.

On my way out, the nurse caught me in the hallway.

"I think you're pregnant!" she said.

"No," I answered, *"It's not me. I can't get pregnant."*

"I'm pretty sure it was you. Let me test it again right here before you go."

"It won't be positive; I can't have babies."

The nurse dipped the test in my cup of pee right there in the hall of the office and we watched the lines change. Our eyes met over the cup.

"See, you're pregnant!"

I clasped my hands over my mouth and sobbed, breaking down in shock and disbelief while the nurse screamed in joy for me, throwing her arms around me. The doctor came out, asking what was going on.

"She's pregnant!" the nurse screamed.

"Oh my gosh, this is amazing!" and the doctor joined our hug circle.

They immediately brought me back into the office for an internal ultrasound and I saw my daughter for the first time. She was just a tiny egg sac, just barely a few weeks old. But she was there.

They sent me for blood tests every day for a week to make sure my hCG levels continued to rise. If I was to miscarry, they wanted to catch it early. To my relief, the numbers rose and the egg sac grew. All of the above is true.

I wish I could say that my pregnancy was a dream but that would be too easy. The first trimester hit me with the heaviest exhaustion of my life, hard, painful breasts, and an acute terror that breathing wrong would result in losing my baby. I was terrified all of the time. In fact, I don't remember much from the first trimester besides fear, blood tests, and a creeping pain that began to settle in my lower back and pelvis. When I told the doctors about the pain, they told me I was experiencing "lightening crotch" although it was a bit early for that and it was nothing to worry about. It was normal. Lots of pregnant people got it. That was partially true.

As I moved through my pregnancy and out of the first trimester the fear of losing the baby gradually began to lift. A new worry settled into me. I couldn't quite place where it came from. Perhaps it was the heaviness of my body, the way I just didn't ever *feel* right. Everyone assured me I was fine; baby was growing well and on target. To me, something felt wrong, but I wouldn't know until years later that while my baby was busy growing, something much more insidious was waking up in my body.

The doctors were concerned I had a mild case of gestational diabetes because I had slightly elevated sugars in the mornings, so I participated in "Gestational Diabetes Bootcamp" and ate a low carb diet and tracked my sugars for the entire second and third trimester. I also injected insulin at night before bed to prevent the higher sugar level in the morning. I was not a fan of the injections, but I dutifully did them every day. I later learned that for some people, slightly elevated morning sugars are normal, and it is called the dawn phenomenon. I still have it to this day but otherwise have perfect sugars.

As my daughter grew, so did the pain in my lower back and legs. So much so that walking became nearly impossible and I was referred to physical therapy for the whole of my third trimester. I don't remember it helping a ton, but I went to every appointment and did all the things I was told. I followed every instruction to the letter and rested at home. I was dedicated to the little girl I was carrying and promised her I was going to keep her safe.

And I did.

Starlight was born through an emergency C-section after 24 hours of labor. When they first pulled her from the hole in my stomach, she did not cry. There was no sound for what felt like forever and my heart stopped right there. But then she did cry and it was the most beautiful sound I had ever heard. They held a blue baby above the curtain briefly before pulling her away. It was a traumatic labor and delivery, and I did not get to hold her for the first hour or so of her life while they put me back together. Instead, they handed her to my husband and told him to take her and leave the room. I laid there, strapped down to the bed like Jesus on the cross and cried while I stared at the ceiling.

When she was finally laid on my chest, it felt like a piece of me had been returned, but in a much more vulnerable way. I understand it now when parents say it's like having your heart walk outside of you. I breathed my little stolen piece of heaven in, and I promised her I would always love her, accept her,

91

work for her, improve for her, be better for her, and be there for her. I reached down deep into the darkest parts of me I have never let anyone see, the dangerous parts that threaten to end me and I surrendered them to her, and I promised that above all, I would live for her.

All of that is true.

Starlight Dreams

I dreamed about you last night.
I saw your curly hair, chrome diopside eyes.
You were laughing
and it was the most beautiful sound
I could ever imagine.
I dream of you a lot.
I don't always see your face.
Sometimes your hair is blonde or brunette,
but it never matters
because you are never out of place.
And your voice?
Oh, is it heavenly!
But the most amazing part is the colors.
My dreams are always dark,
dreary, heavy grays and blues.
Except when I dream of you.
You make everything bright—sunny and airy
baby blues and vibrant greens!
Like real life meets heaven.
You are so, so lovely
and I love to dream of you.
And maybe, if I'm incredibly lucky
my dreams will morph into reality
and I'll finally meet you
for real.

Entropy

Little Starlight

I long for you.
What a feeling,
to long for someone
You never knew,
for someone who
is beautifully new
to ache for such
an innocent
part of you.
I never knew
I wanted you.
But your father
looked me in the eyes
and my heart was
suddenly paralyzed
as my scars grew over
and the heartache healed
and I allowed myself to
finally feel
for real, for the first time.
I saw his eyes
and I realized
how badly I
wanted to see yours.
What a journey it
has been
and what a life
that I have lived.
Little Starlight
I watch for you
every night.

Entropy

And I wait for you
every time
I dream,
to see your curly hair.
I reach for you,
and I grasp at air.
Little Starlight,
don't wait too long,
Mommy's love has
blossomed strong
and I long for you
and your daddy
does too.
I never thought
I'd be missing you
but you'll understand
when you meet
your father.
See, he's the one
who brought me farther
than I ever thought I'd be.
Little Starlight,
when the wind whispers,
follow its words,
follow our slivers
of light through
the dark,
you'll know us
by our hearts.
And we long for you,
Little Starlight.

I Would Wait for You for an Eternity

I thought I felt you,
Starlight,
As the dusk turned into
Evening
As I watched the winter
Leaving
As the snow began
Receding.
I thought I heard you,
Starlight
As the music faded
Lightly
As your father kissed me
Softly
While we walked along
Lake Erie.
I thought I glanced you,
Starlight,
As people swirled around
Me
Blurring colors as they
Hurry
While I wait slowly, writing
Poetry.
I thought I felt you,
Starlight
So if you can read my
Writing
Listen close to words I'm
Weaving
We ache for you, sweet
Darling.

Little Starlight,
Come to us soon.

When You Wish Upon a Star

Dear Starlight,
today was the first day
that I woke up from my fevers and whispers
and missed Mother Nature
for more than two weeks
(for the second time. Or the third time.
Maybe the fourth time.)
And was once again met with a negative line,
and realized
you may never actually come home.
You may always stay a star in the sky
that I look for and sing to each night.
You might always stay a star's light
I cannot kiss and hold tight.
These thoughts have crossed my mind in the past
but I paid them no mind because my mind was set
that you were coming and you were coming soon.
This morning, though,
I realized with conviction
as heartbroken tears blurred my vision
that some women
who struggle to conceive and carry
might have more in common with me
than I have ever been willing to admit.
It's true. But for you,
I will wait until the last possible moment.
I will pray until the answer is definite.
I will hope until I know
because Starlight,
we long for you.
and we are waiting for you
to come home.

Entropy

Before Starlight, There Was Thanatos

I held you briefly,
will never know what took you…
dreams are all I have.

Entropy

Is Anyone Even Listening?!

Instead of counting dreams,
I have started counting pills
to keep track of all the days
it takes to feel something more than ill,
to feel something more fulfilled.
To reconcile damage
until mountains become nil.
To refocus what I hope for
and accept a higher will.

Entropy

Replying "Not Attending" to Baby Showers

I don't know how to be friends
with people who have babies.
There's a hollow space carved into me.
Its name is Desolation.
Its shape is not unlike an egg,
fertilized in bloody lesions.
I suspect this wound will never heal,
it will ache and ooze until I die.
It's a strange scar, a confusing emptiness.
I don't think I wanted more but
I never had the chance to know
and I was ruined long before, anyway.
But I don't know how to be friends
with people who have babies.
I'd like to. I want to.
But your happiness and warmth
drive me to nightmares—
to the pregnancy I lost,
to the one I'll never have.

Entropy

Mistaking Chronic Illness as Impending Death

I suppose in a way I knew what was coming.
I felt the clock ticking as my belly began growing
and for the first time I felt a sort of peace.
A peace about dying.
I suppose I had this peace because now I had a purpose.
A purpose of preparing
and teaching, and leaving things in absolute order
so that my Link wouldn't be broken.
My Link could never be broken.
He needed to be whole and safe
so he could raise
The little Starlight we had stolen from the sky.
And it isn't that I wanted to die,
I just realized that I could.
I realized I could leave like my father before me
and leave holes where there shouldn't be.
I felt the pain growing in my body,
the aching in my joints and limbs,
I couldn't tell you why, I just knew I had a time limit.
An expiration date.
And I would not wait until it was too late.
So I started writing things down,
Started creating a schedule that was easy to follow.
I organized our shelves in an effort to organize our lives
so that should I leave, he wouldn't have a hard time.
Or as hard a time.
My Link.
We made love as often as we could.
We spent more time laughing than arguing.
More time building than destroying.
More time preparing in happiness,
than giving into pettiness or inconvenience.

If I was running out of time,
I would choose how to spend it.
Maybe someday I'll be 50,
I don't know—
And that's the scary part of it,
you never know.
But I had to make sure that when I left,
only the best would remain
that I would be more than a name,
my daughter would know me
and know that I loved her
so she would never have to worry or wonder
where she came from.
So she could feel whole in spite of the hole.
That he could be her Link to me
As he was my Link to love.
I know it sounds kind of cheesy, but honestly
sometimes we need to look at our own mortality
and evaluate the life we are living
and the life we are leaving.
And I hope to God that if I do see God,
those left behind will have more happiness to remember
than regrets and arguments over trivial pursuits
that meant nothing.
I am twenty-eight.
Maybe someday I'll be fifty.
Maybe someday I'll be eighty.
For now, twenty-eight is all I can be.
And I'd like to be living.

To Hold a Galaxy

I stroke my belly thinking
of all the things I've carried
and how you, by far,
are the best thing I've carried
and the only thing
that has brought pain
followed by an absolute promise
of unmeasurable happiness.
And I realize
I must be made of greatness
to carry you
after carrying so much.

Entropy

A Shift in Perspective

The doctor said
she is eight pounds today
and I carry this weight
proudly, but in disbelief
going from "You will never carry anything."
To "Congratulations.
You are worthy after all."

Entropy

My Father's Legacy

Dad,
I hope you know
another part of you
lives on
and another part of me
is no longer stuck
singing sad songs
of longing.
I'll always miss you
but sometimes I feel close to you
because I imagine
how I look at her
is how you
would have looked at me.

Entropy

Knew I'd Love You, Didn't Know if You'd Love Me

Little bits of healing
come in unexpected places
in ways unanticipated
on the tiniest of faces.
Little bits of healing
are worth the pain in waiting.
They outweigh the things
you're feeling
and they make this life
worth living.

Entropy

Seedlings

As I drink my Mother's Milk tea
I look out at my overgrown garden.
I smile as I see that the weeds
have overtaken everything.
However I see my basil is still growing—
in fact, it's flowering
as if it knew it should not wait on me
that I would become too busy
and so it is busy living just fine without me.
Flowering, getting ready to go to seed
to bring in the next generation of sweet basil.
I smile as I drink my tea
because the same thing
has just recently happened to me.
I kept on living,
eventually flowering
never minding the weeds around me
and the most beautiful thing happened:

I became a mother.

Entropy

Love Lived in Me

"Be gentle on yourself," I say as I gaze
into a mirror that is shaming me.
"You just gave birth," I remind myself.
My fingers waltz on an ugly, bumpy
dance floor, raised and broken.
"Be kind," I remind. "You grew so much
Love inside of you, they had to cut you open
and remove it from you there was so much Love
because the world needs it. And you did that.
Give yourself time," I suggest to my stomach,
"Don't worry about being flat or being fat.
You're working on it, and you're doing great.
Don't visit the scale. It doesn't weigh how you're feeling.
And speaking of feeling," I place my hands on my heart,
"It's okay if you feel broken or if you feel stolen,
part of you is walking around outside of you
and it takes time to adjust and feel whole.
Be soft," I tell myself, "There is time to be
what you want to be, and what you want to see.
Don't miss out on being happy
Even when you feel like you're drowning.
Love has lived inside of you–
Did you hear me?
Love has lived inside of you.
How could there be anything wrong with you
when you have created the most extraordinary thing
there could be?"

Entropy

Stop Judging Mothers

The pressure starts in my chest as I survey my house
and the rest of the mess I haven't gotten to yet.
I move to fold some clothes,
become distracted by dirty dishes—
My stomach growls at the thought
of food and my mood takes a dive
as I spy myself in a mirror in a nightgown five days old
crusted in dried milk and sweat and I bet
some baby poop somewhere
because it gets everywhere.
The pressure rises as I sit
at a table fumbling as best as I am able
to quiet my child who is screaming and crying
I feel eyes upon me secretly judging
"What kind of mother is she?"
"Can she not hear her baby screaming?"
I question myself too as the tears brim in my eyes
holding them in when my baby finally becomes quiet.
I sit in discomfort because there is no way I'm disturbing her
I would rather suffer than feel judged.
My husband does not know how I envy him:
When he talks to his friends
when he gets up to pee
or get a drink
or go to sleep
or even breathe.
The pressure builds again as I feel guilty for resenting him
because it's not really *him*: It's his freedom.
I am latched at the side as life passes by
or at least, sometimes, that's what it feels like.
And the pressure builds as I feel lonely and overwhelmed...

But it's funny that way because all that pressure dissipates
When I look down and see my babe
smiling back at me as if I am everything–
No, because I am everything.
The laundry can wait and so can the shower
because in this hour I want time to go by slowly.
I find new strength, a new determination
because in her eyes is the answer to all of the questions
which boils down to one: Am I good enough?
And she says,
"Yes, mommy, you are."

Let Our Children Be Soft

No one prepared me
for how I would change
after childbirth.
That I would become softer
and more forgiving,
be driven to make this world
a better place.
That I wouldn't know *vulnerable*
until another person held my daughter,
that I would become softer.
Softer.
I've spent my life being
Independent
Solid
Stoic
Unreadable
Unmovable
A fortress of emotion
founded on trauma
I have been a compound
of smothered semicolons
and commas,
my tears held prisoner,
hastily wiped away
in the unfortunate event
of an irritating escape.
And now I find myself
Sobbing
over baby clothes
that she has outgrown

Entropy

Weeping
as she falls asleep at my chest
her delicate face wet
with a milk drunk smile
while I remain humbled
in the glow of her existence.
While others have been hacking away
at my fortress of emotional solitude,
my daughter has vanquished it
in one soft motion
and I do not think
I shall ever rebuild it.
My daughter
has made me soft
and I have never felt so strong.

Starlit Lullaby

Sometimes it's hard to sleep
with a little Starlight
so close to me
knowing
that nothing
can compare to the love I'm feeling
when I'd rather look at her
when I really
should be
sleeping.

Entropy

I Believe in Hope Because I Believe in Starlight

If I had kept all the negative pregnancy tests
I could have built a tunnel to the lost city of Atlantis
because its believability is as fragile
as the fertility in my broken womb.

I think about that time I didn't take one
and that maybe if I'd had one
it wouldn't have been too late.
There wouldn't be negative ones
paving the driveway to the cemetery
that I now carry in my heart.

I think about the defeat that crushed my soul—
Another reason why I wasn't whole.
Another life literally stolen from me
by an entity that consumed me at six.

My heart clicks.

I ponder the reasons for the ways of things
and while I've found peace for some things
dark and terrible things still linger when the lights go out.

I remember "I think you're pregnant"
I remember saying no, indignant
at the thought that something perfect
could come from something broken.

If I kept all my negative pregnancy tests
I would make a frame for my daughter
to show her what love looks like after

Entropy

a terrible storm
and she wouldn't see the failure
that I felt before her.
She'd see hope.

I hold her, listening to her even breathing
as I am pondering the path that was leading
down a place built of emotional bricks
each and every negative test worth the risks.

My heart clicks.

I hope she will know faith can endure in the hopeless
that love can grow in the loveless
That every negative test will eventually
lead forward to greatness
and she should save them
and frame them
as a reminder of how far she has come.

I wish I had saved my last negative test
because that was the beginning of the best.

My heart rests.

My Sheets Don't Smell Like You Anymore

My love, the darkness is enveloping
the way your arms once were.
I'm left lying in a darkness
of which we share no more.
I feel her move beside me,
she is stirring in her sleep.
Did you know, she sleeps just like you?
I can tell her sleep is deep.
She is delicate and fragile
but her cheeks are nice and full
and though I love her company
it is for you, I feel a pull.
I miss your touch within the night
when bad dreams cursed my head,
I miss feeling you breathe beside me
as we lay entwined within our bed.
I miss your softness and even your snores
which would frustrate me to no end
but now that they're gone,
my love, my dear, I would welcome them back again.
You're sleeping in another room
so the two of us won't be disturbed
but hearing you walk away from me
is the saddest sound I have ever heard.
I love this child beside me
and I believe nursing her is the best
but that leaves no room beside me,
no more space for you to rest.
And I know you won't be gone forever
this is just temporary, for sure
but the comfort of you is missing–
My sheets don't smell like you anymore.

Entropy

I know most others don't understand
or perhaps think me most dramatic
and that's okay, I don't care what they think
I find it calming to wax poetic.
This transition of life has been very hard
and this bed seems so much bigger
and I can't wait for the day when she is sleeping
and when we can be back together.
It's two a.m. and it's time to feed
as I bring her body closer
and after a while, I'll close my eyes
and dream of you, my lover.

Letters To an Undisclosed P.O. Box

Dad,

I'm writing to tell you about your granddaughter. I know you would just love her. I tell everyone she's a keeper, even if she's not a good sleeper. We are working on it. She'll be five months just before my birthday and she's changing so much, every day. I love seeing the fresh glimpses of personality. Some say she takes after me, some say her daddy. Either way, she's perfect. Link has blossomed into a hallmark father! I love watching them bond together, listening to them share laughter and the contentment that comes after. Sometimes I close my eyes and pretend it's you and me. I'm pretty sure she's started teething, I feel bad for her and for me! Seems there will be no breaks in between my baby becoming a little less baby. But she's gonna look darn cute with little pearly teeth. I can't wait to see her smile. I take pictures all the time, of everything. I think Link gets a little annoyed with me but I told him, from the very beginning that the three of us would be doing everything. We just had family portraits. For the first time in my life, I am all about the stereotypes, capturing all these moments that come by from the 5 a.m. smiles to the splashes at bathtime. It's a pastime as I watch it fly by. She's already a very opinionated little girl. She wants to see everything in her world. She's already trying to speak words. I think she'll have little bouncy curls. I'm not sure about her eyes. I'm holding out pretty good. It's been hard, but I knew it would be. Don't worry, I'm taking care just as I should. I want to be here for everything.

Anyway, I just wanted to update you. I haven't forgotten about you. I think of you every time I see Starlight and Link together. It makes me wonder.

Talk to you soon
Love, your daughter

Entropy

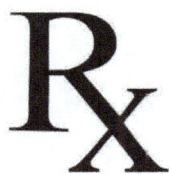

PRESCRIPTION

Patient Name: ~~████~~ RAVVEN

Address: **PLEASE MAKE it StOP**

OTC Tylenol for cramps
Referral for pelvic floor therapy
Exploratory Surgery for endometrium growth,
ovarian cysts
Recommended dilation and curettage
Mirena coil for symptom control

Disorder

Patient referred to nutritionist
for weight loss

Date: 2020   Signature: Doctor

Entropy

After Starlight was born and we settled into the uncomfortable routine of new parents and unlawful newborn, the haziness of existence began to come back into focus and with it came postpartum depression and, you guessed it, pain. The pain that had developed in my lower back during pregnancy never entirely subsided and a dull, throbbing, aching pain had settled into my pelvis post-birth.

I was constantly exhausted. I was reminded that all new parents are expected to be and I was given the incredibly unhelpful advice of "sleep when the baby sleeps". I nursed full-time, a journey that started out with a lot of anxiety. Starlight had difficulty latching and the hospital did not have a lot of support besides "keep trying" and offering formula. A fed baby is the best baby but since so much of my journey had not gone the way I had hoped for, this was the one thing I desperately wanted to be able to do. Eventually she took to the breast, and I was relieved to learn that I was an excellent producer. Nursing and pumping full-time added a new energy cost to my already exhausted body. In the months that followed I shed weight like it was nothing, my body burning through whatever it had on hand in order to keep up with my needs and the needs of my hungry child.

A spasming, urgent, painful bladder came to call. If I had to urinate, I would have to run to the bathroom right away, sometimes multiple times. It felt like my bladder couldn't make up its mind whether or not it had to go. It was stressful and unpredictable—especially with a nursing baby. I was told by countless women that bladder problems were normal post pregnancy. "Bladders just aren't the same after birth." It seemed right to me. The rest of me wasn't the same afterwards. Why should my bladder be any different? I was promised it would "level out" and to invest in some pads for leakage.

The other pains persisted.

At my postpartum checkups I brought it up to my OBGYN and she said it sounded a lot like endometriosis—a diagnosis that had been mentioned just before my confirmed pregnancy. She explained to me that endometriosis is when tissue that is similar to the inside of the uterus grows outside of it, like on your muscles or ovaries, or even in your intestines. They are small angry red lesions that can cause inflammation, scar tissue, infertility, and terrible pain. It doesn't even matter how big or small these lesions are. Even tiny endometriosis spots can cause significant pain depending on where they are located. The only way to confirm it is through laparoscopic surgery.

My doctor wasn't completely convinced I had endometriosis or if I did, that I had a mild case of it. Instead of opting for that surgery right away, she instead suggested the Mirena birth control coil first. She said it was often a good first line defense against endometriosis symptoms because it could control heavy bleeding and painful cramps. She could do the procedure in the office by placing it with a metal rod through my cervix into my uterus (without any anesthesia by the way) and we could be in and out. I trusted my doctor. That is what we do.

I would like to take a moment to acknowledge that the cervix has several hundred nerve endings that have both pain and pressure points. Never in my life did I endure a procedure like a cervical swab or in this case the Mirena coil and walk out of it thinking, *"wow, the doctor was right, it really was just a pinch!"*

We hold vaginas and vulvas and wombs and labia in such high esteem, don't we? We sexualize and glorify them, expect them to be beautiful and delicious, shave them, shape them, market a thousand different ways a vagina should look, smell, taste, feel. Somehow, we still end up shaming the fact that we have one between our legs through odor control commercials, anti-period jokes, and banning our already nonexistent sex education. We sell products to make sure they can be fruitful and multiply but only on a superficial level. When it comes to actual reproductive health, we brutalize vaginas and wombs in the office, gaslight women and femme presenting people's pain and suffering, rely on decades-old research, and ultimately still know so very little about how diseases of the womb work, how lesions like endometriosis come to be. We sit there, with our legs crossed, hoping for a miracle but promised nothing more than whatever the current white, cis man in office believes is worthy for a vagina. And I think we all know what trust fund billionaire politicians think of vaginas and vulvas and wombs and labia, especially when they are underage and don't have a voice.

All of it is revolting. All of it is true.

I got the coil. It was painful. I waited it out. It didn't help. The pain continued to grow. It grew so bad, I had difficulty walking, having sex, even lifting my baby. The weight that I had lost began to return. I was referred to pelvic floor therapy, an act that I absolutely hated. As a survivor of SA, it was traumatizing for me to have strangers put their fingers inside me. I did my best to endure it, and it did help to a degree, but eventually I stopped going for my mental health and because I didn't feel I was progressing.

Throughout this time I had more tests done. I had an ultrasound done of my uterus where I had to go in with a full bladder. Then midway through I emptied it and the technician took more pictures. She was a bit annoyed with me because there was still fluid in my bladder even after I had peed. I remember being shocked because it had felt completely empty to me! On the ultrasound it showed that my uterine lining was 8mm thick when it should have been less than 1mm. This led to my very first cancer scare.

All the cells inside my uterus were growing over and on top of each other instead of shedding like they were supposed to. My doctors were worried about the cells mutating and growing over each other and ruled this as a cause to look for uterine cancer. My doctor explained they were going to use a metal rod tool to go in and scrape and scoop out part of the inside of my uterus so it could be biopsied. It was as painful as it sounds. They did inject some local lidocaine into my cervix, but I still felt everything, nonetheless.

The biopsy came back normal and nobody at this clinic ever said anything about my thick uterine wall and brushed it aside when I asked about it.

While all of this was going on, I was feeling immense pressure from my doctor to decide whether or not I was going to have another baby. In her opinion I had to start trying right away since I had fertility issues and she wanted to get me on fertility drugs right away. Something in my body told me that it wasn't in the cards for me.

I can't even begin to describe the emotional turmoil I was placed in during this time. The societal pressure of people asking when I was having our next baby, the fear of not understanding what was wrong with my body, the anxiety of another pregnancy, the shame of not wanting to endure another one, and the acute exhaustion and pain I just couldn't shake. I felt so incredibly alone during this time. My partner did the best he could, but I will not lie, this was a very hard time in our marriage. I told him more than once that it was okay for him to leave me for someone healthier. Of course, this wasn't the future either of us had planned for, what could we do but hold hands and hope for the best?

Inside I began to wonder who would I be outside this predetermined destiny that had been visualized on my behalf? What if I didn't have more than one child? I would have more to give to her, more to offer her. Then a selfish thought creeped in. I would have more time to give to myself too, something I had never really entertained before. What is a woman outside of a man? Outside of a child? Outside of a womb? Was *I* ...a woman?

I cried and screamed voiceless screams into a sky that returned emptiness. There were never any answers, only more questions and I was tired, so *so* tired.

Eventually the day came that I had my exploratory surgery. I was in pain all the time and I told the doctor explicitly, "Please excise whatever you find, I'd rather be healthy and happy for the baby I have than be worried about what ifs."

It was the height of Covid so Link wasn't allowed to be with me very much as I went out and in and I don't remember a whole lot from the surgery but I do remember hearing the words *"we found it"* and *"we left it"*.

Doctor betrayal should be talked about when it is experienced. Are there good doctors out there? Absolutely. I am very fortunate to be in the care of some excellent doctors in my current timeline. They are good people and I feel heard by them. But six years ago, waking up from surgery and throwing up from the anesthesia, the last thing I wanted to hear was my doctor having done the exact opposite thing I had asked her to do. She betrayed me and I suffered for it.

She did find endometriosis. It was growing happily away on the back of my uterus. Why did she leave it there? She was worried that removing it would somehow impact my fertility, or my ability to carry another baby in the future.

She left me in pain.

With no solutions.

She chose my womb over my health.

My womb over me.

My womb over something I wasn't even sure I wanted or could even handle.

I did not go back to see her.

This doctor's choice altered the direction of my life. It broke through the tiny sliver of faith I still had left in the medical community. I had spent years being fat shamed and shuffled, ignored and looked down on, and here was a doctor I thought I could trust and at the end of the day had I really mattered? She had been pushing me so hard to get pregnant again, I can only wonder if it was some kind of agenda.

I did my own research online and joined Facebook groups for endometriosis. I learned how to manage as best as I could at home. I was extremely depressed and worried about the endometriosis growing inside of me. It could grow anywhere—your spine, your bladder, your organs, and even in rare instances, your brain! I found out that there was one endometriosis specialist in our state. One! And I got an appointment.

This doctor was kind and patient with a shadowing doctor present. He validated my pain, affirming that endometriosis did not need to be large to be painful. He reviewed the previous laparoscopic surgery and he asked why the doctor opted to leave the endometriosis. When I explained why, he exchanged a quizzical look with his fellow doctor and said, "That's…not something we usually see here…" He was careful with his words but I understood what he was saying.

Because of how my pain had progressed, I made the difficult decision to have a hysterectomy. Since the endometriosis seemed to be growing primarily on my uterus, the hope was that it would be less likely to grow back in the next ten years. Another nasty thing that endometriosis can do, even after it has been excised. There was a heaviness to letting go of this thing that allegedly made me a woman but also…

Maybe I didn't want to be a woman anymore. I didn't have a word for it then, but I wanted to discover femininity and joy and personhood outside of all the trauma and expectations that had been handed to me so long ago. I was tired. My uterus was tired. There was a part of me that just wanted to exist between the lines, between the colors. No labels, no expectations, I could just be what I felt and who I felt. But at that moment, the only thing I felt was as if I was breaking in half. On one hand I just desperately wanted to be free of pain and the burden of this womb, and on the other I felt like I was betraying everything I was born to be.

And then surgery day came.

If I had received adequate care oh so long ago, it would have saved me *so much* pain and *so much* emotional turmoil and anguish. The surgery went well and when I woke up, I was met with some shocking news. The endometriosis had spread across my uterus but had also grown over my pelvic floor, and they excised it. There were several large cysts on my ovaries which they removed, along with multiple cysts on my cervix which they removed and sent to be biopsied. They turned out to be pre-cancerous. And my fallopian tubes, which were also removed, were both scarred shut. Oh, and the thick uterine wall? Adenomyosis, a chronic, painful uterine condition.

All of this, and especially the scarred Fallopian tubes, would have made it extremely hard if not impossible to have a second baby. Meaning, if I had let the other doctor peer pressure me into trying, I likely would have been met with even more heartbreak.

In a way, I felt like my body made the decision for me. In some ways it made it a little easier, in some ways it didn't.

I kept my ovaries and healed up over the next year, but I never felt like I ever really fully recovered from either the birth or the surgery. Something was never right again. There were new pains, new aches, and a fatigue that never went away.

One night, I laid down next to my baby and watched her sleep. I stretched out my arm next to her and tapped my pointer finger and my thumb together. A strange buzzing sensation echoed in my fingertips and up my arm. It was new, almost as if my arm had been asleep but not as intense. I looked at my hand curiously, assumed it was just the fatigue, or from holding the baby, and I tucked this new piece of knowledge into me.

I was too afraid to go to the doctor. I was too tired to begin it all again.

And all of this is true.

Textbook Womanhood

The doctor murmurs, obscured by charts and computers.
I wonder what her face looks like as it has yet to see mine.
"It could be this or this or even that," she murmurs.
I am buried, rooted *mycelium* blooming,
piercing eardrums and corrupting my ability to filter
her words from turning into:
"You are broken.
You are damaged.
You are worth nothing."
My heart sinks into a belly that
has forgotten how to eat for love
It is starving for relief,
bloated with decomposing leaves
that had promised to thin me.
I watch her don latex gloves
prepared to invade the innermost parts of me
as if the rot has not already spread there,
as if she could possibly take hold of it,
the root of this great evil and extract it from me,
vines tethered to poisoned veins.
Would I cease to exist?
Would I even know how to live if pain did not own me?
She pushes—cold, wet; squelches—
I clench and cry, burning
from embarrassment, bewilderment,
a body desperately trying to exist.
She's kind, the doctor is.
It's my own mutated mushrooms
that twist her words to poison,
giving myself good reasons to rot.
"Broken."

The doctor retreats, pricked by thorns
that aren't supposed to be growing there.
She suggests a progressive treatment.
I ask her what that means, pulling my legs into me,
blood pooling onto the table
my scarred thighs sticky and bruised—
the only existence they have ever known.
Her response is muffled by traumatic memory.
The drive home is quiet.
Link tells a story as I withdraw.
Overgrown roses contract my uterus
their ill-gotten petals pooling a permanent stain.
I lie to my partner when we arrive at home
and I choose to cry in the silence of myself,
dampening the paper that delivers
a *maybe* instead of a *remedy*.
I have already spent years consuming oceans,
climbing mountains, sharpening my skills
to carve away pieces of myself.
They do not believe me when I say
I would give anything to rise from the dead.
I weigh my options on the scale and
see my depression has scaled higher,
The number distorted by the rot
now running down my leg. I sink.
My lungs are now compressed and struggling,
my heart is racing, my hands are shaking,
Goddamn, what is happening to me?
I can hear Link breathing.
"You have to try," I hear him saying.
"You didn't live just so you could get on with dying."
I tell him he shouldn't have married me.
He says he loves all of me.
I say I can't do this kind of therapy.

Entropy

He says give it time and let it be.
Everything will turn out fine.
I am doubtful as I have heard this line
from every doctor I have ever seen
and still this sickness eats away at me
and still I wonder if it is more me than it,
even as it pools around me, even as it
constricts the soul of me, rooting me.
Forget-me-nots have bloomed from my fingertips
and I offer them, as if I have nothing else.
I have nothing else.
I am broken.

Entropy

Fucking Therapy

I booked an appointment for pelvic floor therapy
and I smiled ruefully because I had always said
that therapy wasn't for me.
Opening up just wasn't my thing,
exposing tender broken pieces wasn't my scene,
if I couldn't be king of the castle, then I would be queen
and these gates wouldn't lower for anything.
I never knew a vagina could need therapy like a heart
that it wasn't my soul but my legs that would part.
I guess when I think back to the start—
Well, it all makes sense.
I grow tense in recollections of my bruised personal space
when he was far too close to my face
when my lips were parted on my face and under the sheets,
starting at age six and up, again at age twenty.
I grew colder as I grew older.
I tried therapy for my soul, I didn't consider
there were other holes that could have used it.
I got married—to a beautiful human by the way.
The kind that reminds you of warm summer days
followed by hot steamy nights,
except for the fights between my mind and my sex
which would often end in tears and he'd hold me near.
If we couldn't have sex, then comfort came next.
Eventually we had a baby
but not without losing our first at the beginning,
so I carried this baby deep in my pelvis
cocooned within a traumatized uterus,
and my pelvis took a lot of stress
until I couldn't walk as the months progressed.
My muscles were tense,
determined to carry this baby to safety.

147

Entropy

And I did. And I did it proudly.
I still consider it a triumph,
even with a C-section after 24 hours of labor.
My vagina was spared, I sighed in relief for her.
There was enough scar tissue inside of her.
Then three months later, I discovered the pain had returned.
I felt burned by the fates.
I resented that pain was the association to sex
instead of what should have been pleasure,
a quaking pool of desire that thrills you and rocks you
leaving you feeling both full and empty—
that's why I booked therapies.
I wanted to undo what had been done to me.
I wanted to be free from the years
of abuse and tragedy.

I never thought a vagina could need therapy.
Perhaps if I hadn't been ashamed
I would have spoken sooner
and someone could have told me
that I needed another kind of therapy.

Life doesn't use lubrication when it fucks you,
leaving microscopic tears inside you
that burns every time love enters you.
We could probably all do with some therapy.

I'll be trying in two Mondays
to open up something that hurts me.

Waiting Rooms

There is something cold and sterile about a waiting room,
a heavy aroma of gloom followed by chemicals and old plastic.
The one I'm currently sitting in is a bracing white and gray
with playful floral paintings, perhaps to
distract from the reason for your stay.
Peaceful pinks and soothing purples,
blues to smooth away the worries.
They remind me of spring, a new season of beginnings.
There's a splash of color provided by
the dusty indoor tree in the corner.
A plethora of magazines, tissues, and pamphlets
Strewn in chaos, out of order, curling pages along the border,
a reflection of how I'm feeling as I
sit in chairs that beg for healing.
The squeaking of the office doors startle me
much like the vibration in my bones,
the anxiety of answers unknown,
a place where pain has grown.
I can hear the chatter of the receptionists
but the words blur together
as I pull myself together, my brow as heavy as the weather.
How fitting I arrived in rain.
I focus on a plain gray and white speckled floor.
My eyes follow the pattern to the door
out of which I would rather be heading.
The office door opens, a nurse beckons,
calling not for me but for another.
I wonder how they feel about being here.
I try to read their face but am forced to look away
because they are too honest in what they say.
My heart hurts my throat as a white coat calls me.
She is kind to me.

149

Her mouth speaks words of encouragement
while her eyes convince me to believe it.
My heart returns to its cavity.
She speaks as she works on me:
"You should work on forgiving your anxiety."
She says I'll never be the same if I can forgive my body's pain.
What a concept, to forgive myself.
Dare I even...*love myself?*
It is only just the beginning, a blush of colors heralding
a tender spring, developing.
And I wonder, will my body always be a waiting room?
Do I dare have hope in white coats?
And do I dare, do I absolutely dare to forgive myself?
"Please," I beg silently. *"I want so much more..."*

Aphrodite

I have seen my fertility
compared to a flower,
a blossoming rose, fragrant lilies.
I have seen my womb compared to a garden,
fresh daisies and petunias,
delicate violets and fragile baby's breath.
It is something sacred and holy
worshiped by the good men,
abused by the bad men,
shamed by other women,
misunderstood by self.
This womb of Bedelias
is capable of extraordinary things,
such as magically transforming
baby's breath into the real thing.
It's something only a womb can do
and this garden of surfinia splendor
is the mark of a woman,
is what makes her a woman,
or at least, that's what I was taught.
How shamefully we prune each other's gardens,
planting seeds that become invasive weeds.

                                        I wonder.

While they are out there
speaking of roses between our legs,
I wonder if they realize
that roses have stems
and those stems have thorns
and those thorns are tearing me on the inside,
massacring my body,
leaving behind scar tissue and bitterness.

What happens when we are forced to
remove those thorns,
and this flower,
worshipped by the masses
is sacrificed in the process?
And this womb,
once fertile and blossoming
is withered and dead
and then...gone.
What am I then?
Is there nothing left of me to celebrate?
I will look at women whose bellies are blossoming,
I will hear people question,
When will my own garden
blossom with baby's breath
and I will have to tell them
"I'm sorry,
I have no garden left."

This Isn't My Body

I don't know how to sit with my grief.
These stagnate waves saturate skin
and my heart beats to a bloody devastation
as though it has never known destruction before.
Hollow chambers scarred with who it wanted to be,
imprinted by a gnashing of teeth promised to me
when I was just a child.
Oh, I am flooded by love never seen
and now I drown in this haunting of my own being.
I feel like a body lost at sea, washed ashore.
I don't even know who I am anymore.
I revolt against this spirit cultivated in me.
I reject this new tendriled philosophy
my anger burning; a human forest fire.
I am charred carbon of who I could have been,
my bones smoldering a new world,
moss slowly redesigning my scarred skin,
burnt and bewildered without and within,
there is so little of me amongst the foliage
of the disease that has come to claim me.
Do not touch me,
kindness disintegrates me.
I have no kindness for myself
as I scream inside hatefully,
adaptive fungus and belladonna replacing
naturally fragile cartilage and tissues
consumptive tears fracture from my soul
and I choke them back, regretfully.
I am reminded, I never learned how to swim,
but I can start a fire, casting ash to the wind.
My footprints leave scorch marks
and I don't know where my tongue is,

poison ivy piercing swollen vocal chords.
Starlight is crying because I am crying
and I scream to my partner,
"Can't you see that I'm trying?"
And once again, I feel as though I am drowning
as grief washes over me
subduing the fire raging wars in my canopy.
What now is left of me?
I don't know how to sit with my grief
but I know I do not want this anger consuming me.
So I sit as a statue. And I grieve.
I attempt to forgive seemingly unending oceans,
mending these scars on my damaged soul
I grieve for all of the ways I've been cheated,
pruning desperate blooms of deadly nightshade
and I try not to hate myself for not
being able to uproot it altogether.
My bones still smolder, an ancient anger
that will never be quelled so long as I live.
But I will learn to live.

I cough.

For as long as I breathe, I will grieve.

For as long as I breathe,
I will grieve.

Nevermind, I guess It Is

Nausea envelops me,
shame lingers, painfully
and I must face the travesty
of a broken heart, regretfully.

Entropy

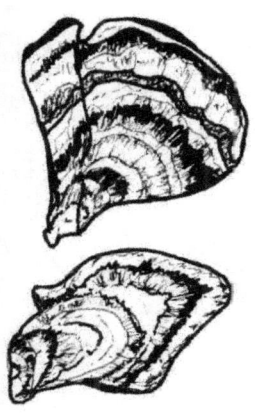

Why Didn't They Find This Sooner?

I struggle to hold myself together
as I watch another piece of me falter
under the weight of this sickness,
silent and deadly, the worst kind of enemy.
It whispers to me, tenderly:
"Sweet ~~girl~~, don't you know
I will rot you from the inside
a slow death invisible to the outside
and every doctor will say you're just fine.
I will decay your flesh as you ponder death
and scar your tissues as you blame your issues
on a past that left you damaged.
Your hips will go out and your head will cave in
And dear, sweet ~~girl~~, in the end I will win."

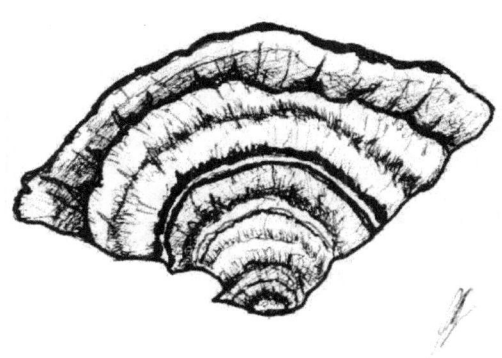

Entropy

I'm Just Being Dramatic

So tenderly I fold the cloth
to hide the blood I've wiped away
my clothing stained by tears I've lost
ripped asunder from the pain
the darkness seeps across my skin
enveloping my aching bones
as if my pores were sweating sin
so many voices and yet, alone.
I turn the shower to boiling hot
shadows steaming choke my lungs
I pause to think of all I'm not
as if hot showers could right wrongs.
but the water trickles off my frame,
there is no sign of suffering.
I will emerge, as if free from shame
though inside, I am slowly dying.

Entropy

Over Iced Mochas and Tylenol

And I wonder, when you're gone,
will I feel empty?
Will I feel your absence deep within me?
or will I hardly notice that you're missing?
Will the sudden ease of pain
just be relieving?
Could my life become full and exciting?
Still, I can't stop myself from wondering,
when you're gone, will I feel anything?

...will I feel empty?

Entropy

I'm a Scorpio, Not Cancer

"But you're so young."
The nurse says to me
as I explain my womb
is no longer blooming,
just a desolation of thorns
silently massacring.
"I know," I reply unwavering.
"I know."

We wait, silent
for the biopsy
surrounded by women
currently creating
knowing I don't belong here,
tears desperately flowing.
"I know," Link whispers lovingly
"I know."

Soon afterwards,
thorn induced cramping
pondering my moonstone
of womanhood beauty
thinking, I have no right to it.
"What are you feeling?"
"I don't know," I weep,
"I don't know.

I think I feel everything."

165

Metaphoric thorns
silently devouring.
Will I come out the same?
I'm afraid of awakening.

How to say goodbye
is an indescribable feeling.
"I don't know," I grieve.
"I don't know."

Still, I Will Reach

And like a phoenix
I will rise from these ashes.

Death, where is thy sting?

Entropy

Dear uterus,

Goodbye.
I thought I would cry when this moment arrived,
but instead I just want you to know
how grateful I am for how hard you tried.
I'm grateful for the child you so carefully nurtured
until my arms could hold her,
how you did not falter as I cried and begged
for nine months to hold on.
Hold on. Just a little bit longer.
I'm grateful for your existence,
for although it has been heavy and pain-ridden,
you produced an absolute miracle
and you showed me what beauty can blossom
when hope and love overthrows trauma.
I'm sorry I didn't appreciate you always
especially on the worst days when all I could do
was breathe and keep moving
as if I had something worth proving.
I wish I had taken more time to accept you
instead of grieving and resenting you.
We are saying goodbye, you and I,
not because I despise you, but because
it's time for me to move on from you.
From pain growing all over you, and the pain attached to you,
when my value was placed in what you could and could not do.
It is time for my Phoenix fire,
to kindle hope and love and to aspire
to bigger and better things beyond
what I could not be growing.
What you can no longer be growing.
But thank you, thank you for giving me
the best miracle I could ever pray for.

169

I imagine you are as tired as I am,
angry red lesions eating away at you.
Eating away at me. Physically. Emotionally.
I think I will still mourn you and what I wanted it to be,
when I was just an innocent girl at fifteen
who just wanted to be loved, completely.
But now I am grown, and I am loved–
I am love–and it's time to let go,
be reborn into who I'm supposed to be.
So I just wanted to say thank you,
but you don't hold my value.
It's okay to rest now, it's okay to say goodbye now,
so goodbye now.
Goodbye.
And thank you, one more time,
for my beautiful Starlight,
for whom I will always choose to stay alive.
Dear uterus,
goodbye.

RX

PRESCRIPTION

Patient Name: ~~xxxxxxxxx~~ RAVVEN

Address: HELP ME, I'm going to DIE

MRI for herniated L4,L5

Tramadol Hydrochloride 50 MG 1 every 8 hours

Methocarbamol 500Mg 1 tablet,

three times a day for 10 days

Decay

Referral for Physical therapy

Increase water intake

Focus on losing weight

Date: 2023   Signature: Doctor

Entropy

In 2023 the unending back pain that had been following me around my whole life took a dramatic plunge. In the fall of that year, it had been ramping up more than usual, and I had been trying to nurse it in between my busy work schedule. Nothing seemed to appease it. One day when I was lifting a tray at work, I moved just the right way and a shooting, burning pain I hadn't felt before radiated through my lower back. I hobbled out of work and at the suggestion of some family members made an appointment with a local chiropractor.

I had seen this chiropractor in the past before. He had seen me for some shoulder pain, taken some X-rays, done some adjustments, and had genuinely seemed to help. I expected much the same. When I showed up for the appointment, I began describing the pain and what led up to it and he immediately went in for an adjustment. I was surprised that he didn't opt for an X-ray, but I did that silly thing I was previously guilty of—I trusted. He did the adjustment and said it was something with the alignment of my hip. He told me to be active, don't sit down for too long, and follow up next week.

I tried to follow his instructions, but the pain felt even worse after the adjustment and by the time the week came, it was pinching and burning in my lower back so badly that I couldn't roll over in bed and could barely lift my leg. It was agony. I was desperately hoping this appointment would fix me. He did the same adjustments again, pulling on my neck, pressing on my hips, twisting my ankles, and afterwards the pain was still there and still terribly wretched. He kept insisting it would get better.

I went home and waited a little longer for it to turn around. To flip over in bed, I dragged myself by my hands and arms, and scooted myself off the bed on my stomach to go to the bathroom. One day in the shower, I turned and something popped in my back and I screamed, falling through the curtain and catching myself on the windowsill. It was the worst pain I had ever experienced, a blinding searing pain shooting through my back and my leg. I screamed for Link but he couldn't hear me until I dragged myself out of the bathroom and threw myself on the bed. When he came back, I was sobbing, begging him to call my brother and take me to the ER.

The two hour wait to be seen was excruciating, and I remember screaming and drooling and crying, "I'm going to die!" all while thinking *"This is the woman they need to see. This is the only way they will take you seriously."*

They did take me seriously and they finally gave me pain drugs and steroids and a scan that confirmed a herniated disc that was squeezing the life out of my sciatic nerve.

I think about that chiropractor a lot, and that if he had taken an X-ray, he probably would have seen a protruding disc. Consequently, he would never have laid a hand on me. He would have referred me to an orthopedic specialist maybe—somewhere before it got as bad as it did. I wish I had advocated better for myself, but it was then that I learned that even familial referrals are not safe from scrutiny. Learning to speak up is hard when you have been taught your whole life to shut up.

After the ER, I followed up with an orthopedic specialist who recommended physical therapy. She insisted the injury in my back was *"not that bad"* and I was young and should "bounce back". I didn't believe anything she said but I decided I would do whatever I needed to fix myself up. I wanted to run after my child again.

I started physical therapy and dutifully followed through, despite the man who made me uncomfortable virtually every visit. He asked me weird questions like, *"Do you believe in angels and demons?"*, *"Do you think people deserve what happens to them?"* and other things. Maybe he was being friendly because I said I wrote spooky books. Inside, my alarm bells were going off. When he looked at me, I felt like a small woman, the kind of woman still good for one thing even if the uterus was dead and buried in the ground.

Eventually I felt like I wasn't getting any better with physical therapy so I stopped going once I had reached my quota. We tried doing a cortisol shot in my lower back. I'll never forget the doctor saying, *"You'll know in three to five days if it worked."* If. Spoiler: It didn't *and* it was exceptionally painful to receive. I returned to my ortho doctor several more times when the pain flared up but eventually she ran out of options and didn't know how to help me. It was time to shuffle me out to the next doctor. She wrote down the name of a surgeon who specialized in disc surgery and said an alternative would be shaving down the part of the disc that was still pressing into my nerve.

The first appointment with this doctor went fine. I had a quick set of X-rays done, he listened and said I could definitely be a candidate for surgery. All he needed was a copy of my MRI to review since it was down at a private clinic outside of the hospital system. It seemed straightforward and I was happy with the way the appointment had gone. I had been suffering with this back pain for just shy of a year at this point and the haunting of that popping pain was constantly a fear in the back of my mind.

At my next appointment, MRI disc in hand, the doctor's attitude was dramatically different. He was cold, abrasive, and talked over me. He briefly looked at my MRI and said my herniation was very small. He then went on to look at my chart

175

on the computer that had not been updated in over a year. He cited my weight and body mass index, saying I was far too overweight for surgery. I corrected him and said that those numbers were not accurate and I had lost fifty-five pounds over the course of the year, but he continued talking over me. He crudely demonstrated that the needle wouldn't penetrate my back fat to get where it needed to be. He had not examined me, had not weighed me, had not listened to me. What had changed since last time? Was it the cane I was using? The pride pins on the bag I was carrying? The makeup I had dared apply that I had left off the previous time? Perhaps the fresh purple and green color in my hair? Or was it simply that he was a surgeon and I was a femme?

I left in tears.

Some friends encouraged me to report him and I did. I was referred to a different surgeon. This one didn't fat shame me but he didn't listen either. In his notes afterward he wrote that the pain didn't wake me up at night even though I told him several times that it did. One thing that all the doctors did get consistently right in their notes though was the numbness and tingling in my legs, both of which didn't make sense to them for such a small, herniated disc.

I was at a loss.

Was this all my life was going to be? Runarounds and shuffling? Fat shaming and misdirection? I wanted to give up. Maybe I could learn to live with it. I watched my child run as she played. I could not run after her.

At the very end of 2024, I got established with a new primary care physician for the sole purpose of getting a referral to pain management. I didn't know what any of it was going to do for me, but it was my last ditch effort. I went in, anxious to get the appointment over with as fast as possible. This newest doctor was kind and patient. She looked over my X-rays taken by the fat shaming doctors and said some of the most validating words I had heard yet:

"No wonder you're in pain, you have facet arthritis all through your spine!"

I was shocked. No one had said any of those words to me. He'd been too busy being cruel than to mention arthritis.

She went on to confirm degenerative disc disease as well and spent time showing me where everything was happening in my back and why I might be experiencing so much pain. When I asked for a referral to pain management, there was no hesitation and I was able to get an appointment in January of 2025.

Things were looking up.

But then, of course, we must look down.

Fifteen years ago, from 2025, the man who abused me, raped me, beat and starved me went to prison. He did not get charged for even a quarter of the things he did to me. Over the course of those fifteen years I built a life for myself and I did my best to heal. I went to therapy, I found and built community, I tried to be a good and honest person, and I chose to fall in love over and over. We move on as we must because there is no other way. But we never really forget, and the body certainly doesn't. And it remembered harder than ever at the dawning of release year.

After a series of localized shots in my lower back, it seemed like we were getting that pain finally under control. There were other things now that worried me. Symptoms that had come and go in the past that had now come to stay. Plus new ones that were emerging, that seemed to grow worse. The vibrations that had started in my hands when Starlight was just a baby had settled into my whole body, traveling all over me in uncomfortable waves. My fingertips would burn from hot and cold sensations. My feet would tingle and burn, my skin would itch and burn or feel like thousands of invisible bugs were crawling all over it. My left side felt weaker and my left hand was clumsier. I would drop things, as if I couldn't hold onto the things in my hands anymore. The clumsiness I had always seemed to have grew worse, with dizziness and double vision that would come and go. But what scared me most was the forgetting.

I was beginning to walk around as if I was lost, all the time. I was forgetting how to do things, simple tasks I had done every day of my life. Words were disappearing and writing, which had always come easy to me, had become grueling and painstaking. Conversations were hard to follow and I would forget them after they were over. I felt like I was going crazy and since it was all invisible, half of the time I was convinced it was psychosomatic!

I started making a list and at my next appointment to the pain management doctor I went down the list. I was shaking, absolutely certain that he wasn't going to believe me because it was all so much and so crazy to me! He listened intently, only interrupting to ask follow up questions. When I was done, he said that I had enough symptoms to warrant a brain MRI and he ordered one on the spot. He didn't even question it. I couldn't even believe it. I was so grateful and relieved—and also incredibly terrified.

On May 1st of 2025 I had my first brain MRI. As I lay there in the tube, I had so many thoughts racing through me. Most of them were me gaslighting myself. Of course the MRI findings would show nothing, of course I would be fine. Deep down, I knew that wasn't true. I knew myself. After all this time, of all the things I had gone through, I knew that this time I had to show up for myself. I had to trust myself. I had to *believe myself.*

Believing yourself when you are chronically ill can be really hard, at least in my experience. I have gaslit myself more times than any doctor and pushed myself more than any outside expectation. I have always been the hardest person on myself and the only person in the room shouting to myself that I am a failure, a disappointment, a regret. I am never doing enough or being enough. Shit is tough out here. And none of those thoughts are true, are they?

I don't think it is any coincidence that my symptoms got worse the year that my abuser got released from prison. I pondered that in the MRI tube, as well. How even after all this time, my body is still carrying the memories of harm done to me and how I will likely never be rid of them. Some growing pains you never really outgrow, do you?

On May 1st of 2025 I also got the results of my first brain MRI. I had multiple lesions on my brain of varying sizes. They were white and looked like little ghost orbs. Fitting for a brain full of haunted memories.

I was immediately referred to a neurologist, whom I wouldn't be able to see for three months. I had no explanations in the meantime, just these haunted orbs on my scans confirming that something was terribly wrong. I started learning what I could about the lesions on my brain, what they could mean, what disease I could possibly have coupled with my vast and many symptoms and one particular disease kept popping up. It began haunting me as much as the ghost orbs on my brain and no matter how many times I refreshed my computer tabs, googled my blood results, or compared my symptoms, it sat there in the fringes, just waiting. I think sometimes, deep down you just know. And deep down, this time, I knew.

One evening, not too far into my three month's waiting period, I sat on my friend Muse's couch and burst into tears.

"I think I have multiple sclerosis," I said.

Home Sweet Haunted Home

We joke and say there's a demon in the house,
cupboard doors wide open, chairs pushed
haphazardly from tables,
various cups of water and old coffee left precariously,
absent-mindedly—
you've never minded my mental illness—
or illness, in general,
I think this is all you have known me as.

When you miraculously found me
in the middle of a black hole sun,
I was already an open cupboard:
exposed, vulnerable, gathering dust.
I was already a half full/half empty cup of water:
forgotten, stale,
particles floating on the surface. Impure.
Never the kind of water gulped for refreshment, nourishment.

But you—you fed me back into the earth;
you poured me into your roots.
It didn't matter what kind of water I was,
to you I was always just water. Life-giving.

There's a comfort to our conversation.
I say things like, *"I'm sorry I leave the doors open,
I'm afraid of being locked inside again."*
You say things like, *"Don't worry, I know it's just the demons."*
I follow up with (sarcastically),
"I'm sorry you are stuck with me."
You follow up with (sincerely),
"I knew what I was getting into."

Entropy

Late nights I cry from the pain.
Early mornings you go to work
to pay for my next medical crisis.
I make you home-cooked meals and
fold your socks and underwear, *sometimes*,
and sometimes the baskets stack
because I cannot lift them.

I tell you things like, *"Someday I'll be rich and famous
and I'll buy you everything."*
You say things like, *"Someday you'll be rich and famous."*
while you patch your work boots.

We laugh and play with our child, so like us, so like me,
I see what I might have been like at her age
if the black hole sun had never shone.
She's loud and assertive and soft and compassionate,
She doesn't quite understand jokes yet so she says things like,
"What do you call a frog in water?"
"What?"
"A frog!"
We laugh for her sake and I say things like,
"I'm so glad you are her father."
You say things like,
"I'm glad she's so much like her mother."

"I'm sorry I can't give you any more children."
                    "I'm happy with our family."
"I feel like I stole your future."
                    "You nourish my roots."

Entropy

You've never blamed me for my illness,
never once shamed me for the cupboards
or the cups or the chairs or the neglected chores,
I can never get ahead.

You just thank me and praise me any time
I accomplish anything.
*"I fed the pets, let the dog out,
and made you salmon for dinner."*

                                    "Thank you lovely, you spoil me."

I have accepted that I will always be a cupboard door left open,
too many things crowd in the dark and
there is no lock in all the world strong enough to keep it shut.
I will always be a stale cup of water,
traces of coffee in an old cup,
a littering of half dreams never fully consumed.

And you—you say you will always have roots
that need water, *that need me,*
and you free me of my confinement
and pour me back into the earth.

Someday, I suspect I will return as a tree.
I suspect you will be a rain cloud.
I will forever be reaching out to you,
and you will forever reach down into me.

"It is always you. Doesn't matter the time or place, or galaxy in space, it's always you."

"It's always you, too, lovely."

"I'll try not to leave the cupboard doors open."

"It doesn't matter, I know it's the demons."

𝔏𝔶𝔪𝔭𝔥𝔬𝔠𝔶𝔱𝔢

My mother acts like I'm dead—
or perhaps like I never existed.
She does not ask my siblings after me,
does not mention or speak of me.
I've been erased from her entire vocabulary.
I wonder how that's working out for her.

I cannot fathom erasure of history,
pretending someone didn't exist and love me.
I still think on people past from time to time.
Memories of when things were once fine,
before the drifting or crossing of lines.
In some circles I still ask after them.

I still ask after my mother,
getting scraps of insight from my brother.
I will never speak to her again, I know.
I have buried and mourn my semblance of hope.
I am better for it. I will heal. I will grow.
I tell myself she is deserving of forgetting.

I am dead to my mother.
I am glad I'm not like her.

Entropy

They Said It's Just Anxiety

I couldn't move—
sleep paralysis cementing
screaming joints, wrists folded into me.
A five a.m. surprise and
all I could move were my eyes,
ears barely registering
a world moving on without me.
So I laid there and I waited.
And I cried.
When I did move,
I snapped and popped and moaned
like a rusted door left locked and alone
barring secrets never meant to open.
"Open up my eyes," I scream.
I have done far, far harder things.
This is all just a bad dream—
but I know a nightmare when I feel one
and I'm not sure I have
ever hurt so badly.
Will I ever not feel his hands on me?
They call it degeneration.
(complex memorization)
Is it the soul that is broken?
I feel para—
my body barely moving around me
Chronic illness, chronic reality.
Who needs a demon for haunting
When evil already resides in me?
I ca—
      n't
         mo—

187

Entropy

Chronic Illness

I feel I am forever trading
pieces of myself on the black market:
A shady, unsterile payment to Life.
Give me the scalpel,
I will slice my body into pieces
to render you my pound of flesh.

The first transaction
became a monthly occurrence
and I wrote checks in blood and tissue,
so much, so heavy,
I wondered when I would bleed out.

Would that it were that easy.

The next settlement came as lesions,
bleeding, festering sores
that chewed and gnashed my insides
bit by bit, organ by organ,
but that was not enough—
so it consumed my first child.

Interest began accruing
and it came as chronic pain:
swelling joints and aching muscles
a buzzing vibration in my bones
phantom pains to remind me
that I was broke and overdue.

Entropy

I was alive but the cost was dear:
First my gallbladder,
then my uterus, my cervix,
my fallopian tubes—
these left bigger cavities in me
than the teeth and bits of jaw
I cut out and traded in at the pawn shop.

And then a few exploratory evaluations,
to determine just how much I was worth,
how much more could I pay?

So costly
for an already shortened life span.

Hand me the scalpel,
dulled from repeat use,
smeared in decomposition.
My payment is soon due
and I cannot afford
to lose my arm or my leg.

I'll take drugs to numb
what is left
and operate myself.

Ataxia

It wasn't always like this,
or was it?
A visceral cracking and popping,
not unlike an ancient willow
groaning beneath a storm.
Not unlike stones worn down
to nothing, pitted like chewed
skin bruised and peeling.
A lurching, haggard beast
long and spindly—
Give me wolf sight and slackened jaw
and I shall be complete.
When I scream,
it's a shrill wind over a
barren and muddied moor,
and when I tear my at skin
clawing for this rapid heart
bent on beating to eruption,
it is pools of dew collected
atop a starved desert flower.
It is a shifting of bones and marrow
beneath an unforgiving human form,
a primal, sickening, twisted perversion
soaked into the fabric of me.
It goes by many names:
Pain. Panic. Punishment.
It is me and I am it.
It twists me, suspended in a
traumatic and vengeful suspension.

It wasn't always like this, was it?
Claws and teeth gnashing out of me—
a sickness that will fester
until it destroys me.

When the doctor handed me my newest diagnoses /

degenerative disease
I held the papers in my hands /
joint deterioration
and briefly dissociated /
likely trajectory
to a time when I was much younger /
physical therapy
a time when I was much healthier /
future surgeries
to a six-year-old me /
pain management
and she was holding papers, too /
joint swelling
we locked eyes, she and I /
chronic inflammation
my friends say I'm taking this well /
you will not get better
but what they don't understand /
linked to trauma
is that I already saw this /
childhood development
I knew something was coming /
malnutrition
I just didn't know when it would show /
the body never forgets
and here, now, it has finally arrived /
the body never forgets
I pick up the pieces of myself that I did not break /
the body never forgets

Entropy

Demyelination

Some days are okay,
I think it cannot be that bad.
I laugh and it vibrates to my fingertips
and in a moment, I forget why I was laughing.
I search for it, travel the neuro networks
eaten by *mycelium* and lose myself—
where am...
what was I...
I describe it like a coffee filter.
Information drips in and percolates out
and it is so, so incredibly bitter.
I feel the numbness travel over me and
every single time I wonder
What will you take this time?

Entropy

Cognitive Dysfunction

Over curly fries and unspecified sticky floors
we decide I shouldn't drive anymore after today.
I become confused easily, my reaction time is too slow,
my body too unpredictable.
I swallow my pride around bubbly Dr Pepper
and attempt to hide the disappointment
that was rapidly turning to panic.
When I was a child I was complacent in my
sufferings, *who was I to know any better?*
In my teens I realized there was so much more
and when I finally broke free at nineteen
I promised myself to never be trapped again.
My leg spasms under the table.
It travels up to my thigh and buttocks
pausing slightly before sending an
electric shock up my spine to my elbow.
I shiver, skin crawling with invisible hives.
The ivy in my ribcage constricts and I think,
Who am I to breathe anyway?
The numbing prickles make it to my chin,
to my lips, to my brows, crawls across my brain.
Nineteen-year-old me would be so disappointed.
I fought so hard to get out and
here I am, trapped inside again.
I roll the Dr Pepper on my tongue.
It doesn't taste like it used to.

Entropy

Do You Still Love Me?

I wish you could tell
when you are burning out
the people you love
because I have never been so afraid
of answering the question
"How are you today?"

~~I am not well~~
~~I am not well~~
~~I am not well~~

~~Will you stay in bed with me?~~
~~I know you can't but~~

~~maybe just a little longer~~

~~how much longer will it take?~~

~~Four doctors and 50k later~~
~~will there be answers?~~

You move away from me
in the bed because I'm burning up
I'm burning up inside

How do you tell
when you are burning out
the people you love?

Entropy

Dysesthesia

Last night I must have forgotten
to toss and turn the correct amount of times
to disrupt the root systems invading my joints.
I wake bleary eyed and fatigued,
weed the overgrowth from my bed
elbows, wrists, ankles, and hips
burning and squeezing from the agony
of poison ivy inflammation.
One arm has gone completely numb
so I sling it over my chest and wait.
Below me, my legs twitch uncontrollably.
My toes tingle, thorns piercing my soles.
My skin itches. Then burns. It travels across me.
I turn my head and all goes blurry.
I sigh and my heart palpitates.
The numbness fades, the twitches subside.
The poison ivy does not. It never does now.
Everything else comes and goes.
Finally I am able to rise and I take my pills.
Some mornings they feel too heavy.
Starlight greets me. She is radiant and beautiful.
Her energy is limitless.
I do not know how she came from me.
She giggles at my forget-me-nots.
I know I'm smiling even though
I can't feel it.

Entropy

Main Street

You tell me to put down roots,
to seed your home with my existence,
to take up space dangerously
even though I know it is temporary.
I am a potted plant in your apartment
you will slowly forget to water.
I was never meant to be permanent,
Or am I? But—
if I depart from under yellow lights
and awkward borrowed spaces,
you will forever be sweeping
away the pieces of me left behind.
Crumbled leaves and desperate petals,
brown capped mushrooms on baseboards:
the parts of me that bloomed
because I hoped it would be enough.
The parts of me that died
because this love existed conditionally.
You will never fully rid yourself of me,
you cannot weed with your eyes closed.
You will be another *mycelium* memory
forever destined to rot inside of me.
What a tangled, bitter root we seed
when first we promise:

"I will not leave."

Entropy

Ocrevus

Hair holds memories," I whisper
watching threads and bundles fall away
each time I run my hands through locks.
Each time water and soap rinses away
depression rot and withered leaves.
Each time my brush smooths curls,
attempting to train them over balding patches.
Which memories are they taking with them?
Are they the words I can't find?
The names of the people I love?
The tasks I have done for near *centuries*?
Why am I left with the timeline
I worked so hard to leave?
Why won't it take those memories
and leave me to pink fogs?

*Leave me naked but dear god
please leave me loved.*

Entropy

When You Wake Up, I'll Be There

How do you see me
when I am in your bed?

Flesh, bones, skin, teeth?
Supple renderings for hardness?
Bury yourself in me,
you know I have the answers
you have so desperately been avoiding.

You kiss around me,
leave purple bruises on thighs
and swollen nipples
and I beg you to hurt me tenderly.

For a moment we are suspended
and I am separated.
I am not sickness or body or breath.
You are more than musings of a
wild and wandering heart.

We may never be more.
We may never be less.

I see you as everything,
just so you know.

I always will.

The *mycelium* will not
take that from me.

Entropy

The breakdown happens in real time.

I won't see it coming,
it arrives under the guise of fatigue…

I'm just tired.

The repetitive task of the last hour
is first interrupted by   pauses.

Wait.

What.
        Comes.
                Next?

~~Blurred lines.~~

I am just tired.

My leg spasms under the desk.
I shudder,
the fog settling heavier.

I am alone now.
I have always been alone.

Tasks I have done for years
I forget in moments.
I suffocate on inevitability
and scream on emptiness.

What have I become?
Where did I go?

Please come back.

Silence.

Entropy

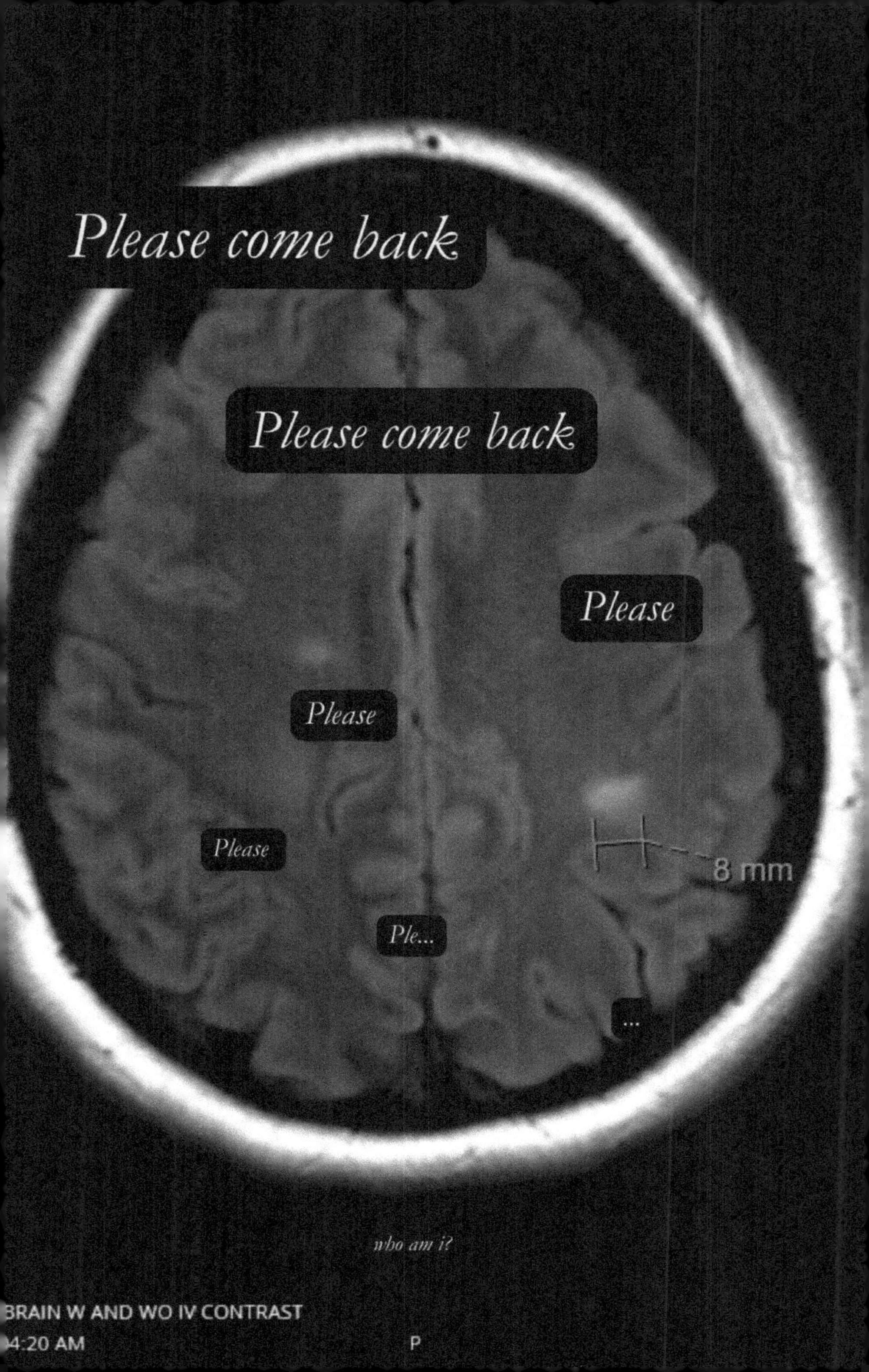
Please come back
Please come back
Please
Please
Please
Ple...
...
8 mm
who am i?
BRAIN W AND WO IV CONTRAST
4:20 AM
P

Entropy

Executive Function

I am afraid there is not
enough of me left this time.

I have spent my life
uprooting this sickness,
these festering lesions of traumas.
It is so exhausting.

Here I am at the precipice again
and I can no longer
tell myself apart.

> *Oh god please why have you abandoned me?*

Is there enough left of me?

> *I am frantic!*
> *I am frantic!*

I teeter on the edge
and those whispers that
began in my youth

become

screams.

Entropy

For All of My Life, I Will Grieve

And all at once I am unearthed,
a grave of moist soil plowed under and over,
splintered bones bleaching under your gaze.
How long have I been broken?
Shrouded, I mourn, gut-wrenching sobs
disturbing the sparrows come to forage
for the worms birthed by my disturbance.
I attempt to gather these slivers of me,
further wounding myself in the process.
I turn this way and that way in desperation,
orbs of agony pooling from topaz eyes that
turn the dirt into mud, attempting to sow me.
Sometimes there is no softness.
Sometimes there is no peace.
Sometimes there is just pain and ugliness
and a sadness so profound it can do nothing
but grieve.

So I grieve.
I hold my slivers, even as they cut my palms.
I remember who I was.
I do not know who now I am.

Entropy

From Cradle to Grave

On this day, thirty-some years ago,
a twenty-two year old father
left work to retrieve a crib
for his daughter, who was due that day
(but who would be seven days late,
prophetic in that I would be
eternally late for everything).
He did not make it home.
He did not even make it to the crib.

On this day, thirty-some years later,
I light a candle beside his picture
and listen for a voice I have only ever heard
muffled from beyond the veil,
from the other side of the womb.
I have spent most of my life feeling trapped
behind a veil, behind a barrier, separated
from the muffled sounds of
who we could have been.

I flex my fingers in empty air
wondering if he is reaching for me,
If the shadow of my grasp will cross over
and meet the shadow of his.
I close brown eyes that refract his initials and
search for him, search for anything.

I even search for my mother, knowing she's
still alive and breathing but somewhere
beyond this barrier, somewhere beyond me.

Entropy

I have never learned how to carry this grief,
I have only ever learned that it will never depart.
It is the unfinished business of a man who
never came home, and the confusion
of a little girl who was never quite enough.

The candle extinguishes, the smoke dancing
with custom made finger puppet shadows.
I sit and listen to muffled sounds.
I wonder if either of them will ever be proud.

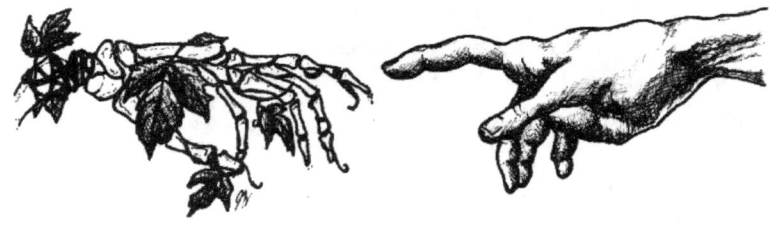

220

We talk of many things.
Politics and wars and identity.
Knives and scars and men in prison.
First loves and poison ivy thighs—
real talk that transcends, gets you high.
We share a brain cell, you and I.
I value that cell, my one cell
void of corruption and pollution.
It travels too far and too fast
for the creeping poison to hold it.
Last night we talked of happiness
and if we have really held it.
I did not have the guts to tell you
That deep down, if I was honest,
I am not sure if I have ever known
what it tastes like, if I've ever truly felt it.
I just listened because I wanted
to hold the things others haven't.
You deserve it.
We may not get all we want out of life,
grand dreams of better things.
"Pick me!", *"Choose me!"* we scream
into a universe far too busy to listen.
But I promise you one thing,
my precious companion,
my brain cell connection:
you may not know real happiness
again in this lifetime
but *I promise you will always
know love.*

Entropy

Bear Witness

The worst, and best part, I think, is watching
everyone around me finally start to get better.
Flowers are blooming for my brother
not on the headstone,
but in the gardens, in his cheeks.
Lily of the valley is in his soul now.
I am glad for it. He has worked so hard for it.
Even Muse, in all his hyper fixations
and unrequited apartment plants
is putting his life together.
I sit quietly, surfinias twisting
around ankles, forget-me-nots
blooming desperately from fingertips.
I'm waiting now. I don't know how to tell them.
I don't know what to say to anybody.
I can't even comfort myself
without falling to despair,
watering the moss and vagrant memories
that feed unrepentant mycelium
oh mother, oh father you have done this to me.
A day passes. And then another.
I can't remember where I was going
when I started this poem.
The lesions have taken that from me.
I watch everyone around me get better
and I know, in my soul,
I likely will not.

Not like them.

Entropy

Sometimes Generational Gardens Should Die Off

Playing catch up was always futile.
I was born rootbound in graveyard dust.
My mother's grief replaced my
white blood cells and
my father's absence ate across me,
presenting as white matter demyelination.
"One day at a time," they say.
Evening primroses for those who
  do not house my vibrating bones,
    do not seduce my lovers' lips on numbed skin,
      do not exude exhaustion by merely
        breathing.
They do not feel my body decomposing from
  fungus webbed wet across lungs,
    thorns grinding cracked bones,
      poison ivy choking swollen joints.
Some part of me was born
prematurely returned to the earth,
my resilience marked as miracle
rather than recognized as tragedy
leaving me rootbound
instead of properly weeded.
A cacophony of blossoms and bitters
  I am everything and nothing,
    the beginning and the ending,
      living and deceasing.
But I think mostly I am horror
because in all of this I am still kind
  and it is still invisible
    and I am still rootbound
      and there is nothing you can do about
        it.

Still, I

Reach

Entropy

No Relapse, No Remission

I thought about my mother yesterday
after a family friend left an emoji on my
brain lesion Instagram reel.
I feel a lot of everything and nothing these days.
Numbness takes toes, fingers, patches of skin.
Sometimes it's replaced by a relentless itch,
other times by a cold so harrowing it radiates
out of the blankets as if I were a block of ice.
And yet still I melt down so easily,
overstimulated constantly,
tears playing a dangerous game of dodgeball
on a lash line smudged in black.
I broke the rules and asked my brother,
"Does she ever ask about me? Ever?"
I forgot I was dead to her so
there isn't anything to ask about, not anymore.
The brain lesions are just my body decomposing
the little bits of me that are left.
I wonder if anyone will tell her.
I hope they do not.
My mother lives and runs in patterns
that ripple in traumas and chased forgiveness.
I will not rise for her on the third day,
will not save her from
the damnation of her choices when I am
trapped in the damnation of them myself.

227

Entropy

The Contract

I am the weathered notebook
scribbled thin with lead and heartbreak.
"Grief and stardust," I tell him.
"The beginning and the ending."
That is my story.
A woven tapestry of embered oranges
bedridden blues, and unrequited purples.
Roses and sunflowers and poison ivy
wrapped around ankles and wrists
that long to dance and entangle sheets.
Kiss me. Hold me. Tell me I am something.
"Grief and stardust," I remind him,
tracing a future tendriled in teals and gray.
Will I be here when you wake up?
My mind strays and I lose myself in lavender.
I breathe in greens, cedar and hope:
Forests of copper mushrooms because of course
he is there when I wake up, no matter where I am.
What a cruel fate, grief and stardust.
Tied to the earth, returned to the stars.
Forever torn in half, sundered by the heavens.
Wholeness has never belonged to me.
Does it belong to anybody?
My pages crumble, pale skin marred in red.
If grief was a color, it would be a galaxy.
I suppose that's why I am made of both.

Entropy

Primary Progressive Multiple Sclerosis

I plan to enrich this world
for as long as I have left.
As pieces of me fall away,
I will sow them into your soil.
I will seed myself into your life,
bury sloughed off epidermis in your garden
marked by phalange and tibia.
I will be so very kind and so very soft
that you will mistake my fatigue as gentleness,
my breathing exercises as calmness,
rather than winds meant to disrupt the violent
wars thundering in the chambers of my heart.
I will not let festering lesions
inflame my senses to bitterness.
My fingertips bloom forget-me-nots,
pushing past anxiety chewed cuticles
and calcium rippled nail beds.
I pluck them for you and place them in a vase.
The world will bloom with pieces of me
for an eternity after I am gone.
I have made it so.
I hear your keys in the door lock and
I quickly wipe the bloodstains from the counter.

Entropy

PRESCRIPTION

Patient Name: ~~█████████~~ **RAVVEN**

Address: **It WAS never in my HEAD**

PCOS
Endometriosis
Adenomyosis
Ovarian cysts
Pre-cancerous cervical tumors
Scarred fallopian tubes
Hysterectomy and ablation
Elhers Danlos syndrome
Dysautonomia
Degenerative Disc Disease
Facet Arthritis
Levoscoliosis
Degeneration of sacroiliac joints
and pubic symphysis
Primary Progressive Multiple Sclerosis

Diagnosis

Date: **over ten years**   Signature: **Doctor**

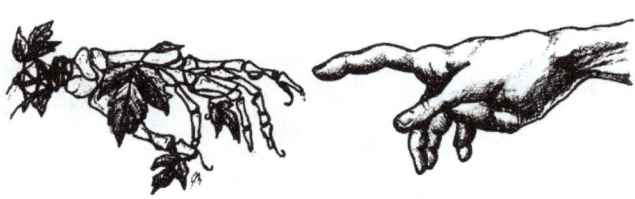

Entropy

The first neurologist I saw had me repeat my brain MRI, this time with contrast, and added on thoracic and cervical spine MRIs. His opinion was indeed multiple sclerosis, we just had to prove it with certainty. We talked about my symptoms, which had become extensive. When I expressed concern over my cognitive decline, he brushed it aside stating that MS didn't cause cognitive issues, it was likely just fatigue and if we fixed my fatigue, we would fix my brain fog.

I left the visit feeling simultaneously overwhelmed and underwhelmed. There was so much new information to take in and a new life I was not at all prepared for. I had tests lined up for me to finally prove this illness that I now knew had been disrupting me for years. And I was grateful for that. Something was still bothering me though. I knew my body and my mind. I had dealt with fatigue for years and had managed to accomplish incredible things: writing books, building a company, raising a child. This new decline felt different. I wasn't satisfied with his answer.

I did the MRIs and scheduled my next appointment to follow up on them and was horrified to learn it would take another three months. I felt myself actively declining as the time had been passing. My mobility had significantly decreased, my "brain fog" had gotten worse, and my daily symptoms were borderline unbearable. It felt like my body was in active entropy, and I was so incredibly scared. I could feel that I was on a countdown that didn't have time to wait three months for a concrete diagnosis.

I am fortunate to live near a city with a top ten MS center and I was able to transfer my care there and be seen immediately. I had two neurologists do my intake. They reviewed my MRIs and discovered I had developed a new lesion during the three months I had been waiting to be seen.

I remember feeling a cold chill run through me. All those months I had felt like something was wrong. I had felt myself deteriorate more. And here was proof that I wasn't wrong. The body doesn't forget. The body doesn't lie. Most of the time we don't understand what it is trying to tell us, but it's always screaming out the truth, begging someone to bear witness.

There were more things I had to do. A spinal tap for one, which was not fun. As someone with Ehlers Danlos Syndrome, injections like lidocaine do not work on me like they do for regular people. My tendons and tissues just don't hold the medication as well so every injection, every needle is always painful no matter what. I felt the needle go into my spine, and I felt it pulled back out. I had so many trips to the hospital that I began to create a magic system for each doctor or nurse I encountered. Vampires at the blood draws, ghouls at the MRIs and X-rays, werewolves at physical therapy, sirens in psychology. It helped me cope with all the new things I had to do.

And I still had a bit of a wait before I could start treatment. I had to get the chicken pox vaccine because I had no immunities, which is a live vaccine and administered in two doses. That means I had to wait two weeks between doses and then another two weeks before starting infusions. In the meantime, the weather got colder and my ability to walk got worse. I struggled with dizzy spells just turning my head, paired with double and blurry vision. I was then sent to an ophthalmologist and while his technician was kind and thorough, the doctor himself was not. He came into the room, examined my eyes, and proceeded to tell me I had optic neuritis and nerve damage in my left eye. The vision loss and problems in that eye were permanent and would only worsen. He told me to get on with my life and learn to deal with it, all with barely looking at me. Then he went on a tangent about how you can't really know if you have MS or not until you are dead and they cut open your brain. He wouldn't give me my glasses prescription even though I had astigmatisms that would have been helped as well as farsightedness in my right eye. I was crying and traumatized by the end of the visit. I talked to both my psychologist and neurologist about his behavior, and they agreed it was inappropriate on his part and gave me resources to report him. Later that night, Muse and I surfed the web and found reviews for the ophthalmologist and they were damning—and they were all from women. He had a long history of dismissing women, being rude and obnoxious to women, and talking down to women. Still, he remained at his place of employment, regularly treating all patients. I wish I could say I was surprised at our findings, but I wasn't. I knew those complaints would be there. He had worked his job for his whole life, earned his tenure, and could continue to do and act and speak as he wanted to. Because he could. Because he *always* could.

Besides the optic neuritis putting me off balance and blurry, the pain in my legs had increased. Some days it felt like my feet were burning. Other days I had perpetual numbness in my left leg. Spasticity came to call behind my right knee. Coupled with my back pain and daily fatigue, walking became painful and exhausting. I dreaded doctor appointments at the big hospital that had a zip code all to itself. I couldn't afford an electric wheelchair, and I wasn't sure if my insurance would cover for one. My hearts took care of that for me, arranging a gigantic book raffle that inspired other raffles online, each dollar going to a wheelchair fund just for me. In about two weeks, they had raised over one thousand dollars to buy me an electric wheelchair so that I wouldn't have to dread all the walking, so I could still participate in walks with my daughter, so that I could have more of a life outside of the walls of my home. I am so eternally grateful to every person that shared and participated and helped change my life. Insurance only covers one mobility aid every five years, so if you get a cane or a rollator through them, that is all you are allowed for five years, no matter how far you deteriorate in the meantime. The generosity of my bookish community bought me a wheelchair and will allow me to get extra assistance through my insurance as I need it. I'll never forget this kindness.

Besides the tests, I started going to occupational, physical, and speech therapy. I was amazed by all these resources made available to me, to help me navigate my new disabilities. In many ways I felt like a fraud at my various therapies because I saw people worse off than me. I felt like I had to "get worse" as if the months of pain, losing my ability to socialize, and losing strength and dexterity in my left side were not enough. I expressed that to my occupational therapist and she was so kind. She reminded me that everyone's journey is different and I shouldn't ever compare. My journey doesn't take away from anyone else's and theirs doesn't take away from mine. We could all learn from that. She asked me what my goal was for therapy that day, or if I had one. I looked away from her because I couldn't face my disease yet.

"I just want to know I can be somebody outside of this," I whispered to her.

During this first visit to occupational therapy, we measured the strength of my hands and arms. My right measured at seventy, which was the normal measure for someone like me. My left however, measured in at barely twenty. My whole left side has been compromised the most during this progression. My left side is weaker, my left leg and foot is numb, my left eye has optic neuritis, and more recently I have noticed that my left eyelid falls just a little more than my right. Sometimes my left hand doesn't respond right away. I can look at it, waiting for it to do the action I am thinking of. But everything all around is slower now. I walk slower, move around slower. I speak more slowly to try not to slur my words. I take longer to process information because my memory and processing doesn't work the same anymore. I began by forgetting little things easily and now it has progressed to big things like the way I fold my hair up after I wash it or the family dumpling recipe I've made from scratch, practically blind, over a thousand times. Sometimes I reach for core task memories and they are just...gone. As if they were never there to begin with. Like a piece of you left while you were sleeping and you didn't get to see it off or say goodbye or make sure it had enough to eat before it left. It's brutal and cold and "terror" cannot begin to encapsulate the emotion behind it.

On August 27th, 2025, my abuser walked out of prison, and I was trapped in my bed after my spinal tap. For the first time in my life, I started having panic attacks about leaving my house or standing too close to the open door or window. I crawled into my bed, my body aching from shots and trauma and did not know what to do.

I was still in bed when I received the official diagnosis via virtual appointment on September 12th, 2025. Primary Progressive Multiple Sclerosis. I thought back so many months ago to the spring when I cried on my Muse's couch. Once my symptoms had started, they had never really stopped and now they were progressing very fast. It was scary. It was devastating. Little by little, pieces of me had begun to disappear and I had no way of knowing if they were ever coming back.

I stayed in bed most of September. I wanted to get up. I wanted to find a way to matter, to live, to breathe. But everything was so suffocating that I did not know how to do that. The only thing I knew how to do was cry. As a person who had always held themselves together, I did not know what to do when I finally fell apart. I was afraid if I stepped outside of my room, that I would be crushed by everything waiting for me. I had a family to tend to, a business to run. People needed answers and I had nothing to offer them.

I found myself slipping into thought patterns like "maybe it would be better if I wasn't here", "maybe I am too tired to fight it this time", "it would be easier and cheaper on my family if they did not have to care for me", "it would be so much better if I did not wake up".

These are scary thoughts to have, especially when you are alone and broken and cannot get out of bed. Haunted pieces of trauma that laid dormant for years sprouted in the darkness of my depression. I had worked so hard for my life, had overcome so many hard situations, fought and scrapped and bled for everything I had. And now, here when I should have been living the best years with my daughter, enjoying adventures with my hearts and husband, I was trapped in a progressive nightmare that was only going to get worse. Everything felt like it was falling away from me. That *I* was falling away. However, many years ago, I promised a tiny little baby that the darkest parts of me belonged to her and I have never been one to go back on a promise.

For the first time in my life, I chose to ask about antidepressants and spoke to my primary care physician and then the psychiatrist on staff at my clinic. We worked together to find a good combination that would help not to take the depression away but get it to a point where I could function again. I was taught many harmful things about antidepressants when I was growing up. That my faith wasn't strong enough, that they made you violent or, on the other end, they made you lifeless. That once you started you could never stop. That weak people only took them because they didn't want to do the actual work to get better. I didn't believe all those things. But I was worried about "losing my spark" and my sex drive so I chose to educate myself, ask for opinions from trusted people, and make a decision for my own health and wellbeing. Freedom to make decisions for our own health and bodies is a right we all deserve no matter who we are. I am so grateful for access to those medications because they helped to bring me back from a very dark and dangerous place. I didn't want to disappear. I very nearly did.

I think disappearing is what I was, and still am, afraid of the most. I had worked so hard to become who I was. I had reinvented myself so many times, been forced to rebuild myself after so many emotional destructions. Here I was again, watching myself be washed away and I could do nothing about it. I couldn't even predict when it was going to happen.

For my entire life, I had been the one in charge, the one everyone came to for answers and help, the one people looked to as the role model and the exception. I was the strong one, the voice of reason. I was the heart of the home. And all of a sudden I lost my independence, my voice, direction, and my stability. I couldn't drive myself anymore. Conversations were difficult and confusing. Just walking from one room to the next was exhausting. And just as upsetting were, and are, how fluctuating the days would be. Some days were pretty okay. Other days were not okay at all. But really, the pretty okay days were spent making up for the not okay at all days, which just caused more not okay at all days...it's a vicious cycle.

We are finally approaching the end of the book. There is no poetry after this because there are no pretty words to soften the blow of this cruel and heartbreaking diagnosis. I haven't been able to write like before. Something has been fundamentally broken inside me, and I don't know if it will ever be fixed. I have finally started my infusions and right now I am on Ocrevus. In May of 2026 I will have more imaging done and we will see what and where new lesions have formed and if any of my older ones have grown. Then, in about a year, we will be able to know if Ocrevus is working for me. It's a lot of wait and see for a disease that has no time to wait.

My hair began to fall out after the first dose of Ocrevus. I had read about it on forums so I was prepared, but I still cried in the shower as I held a fistful of hair the first time. My hair has always been very important to me. I grew up not being allowed to cut it or color it. I had to hide it away under scarves and head coverings. It would be grabbed and yanked as punishment or to get my attention. As an adult, I cut it short and started coloring it. Eventually I grew it out again and colored it purples and blues and greens. A galaxy not fully understood. I couldn't face seeing my favorite colors fall out so I went to my stylist and she cut it short again and dyed it a rich red and black. I am still losing hair. I still cry in the shower.

I wish I could end it all on a positive note. A happy ending, a pretty bow, nice and neat. Chronic illness just isn't like that, no matter what kind you have. And this book wasn't ever meant to be nice or pretty or positive or kind. It's supposed to horrify you, to make you feel uncomfortable; to make you bear witness. To make you feel seen. Validated. Understood. It's meant to be terrible and beautiful—chaos descending into disorganization and decay.

Maybe I will write another book someday about life after diagnosis. About infusions and therapy and relapse and recovery. Right now, it is January and I am filled with entropy.

I look over my charts from years past and I see the abysmally low vitamin D, the ever high white blood cell count, and all the other warning signs and I wonder why no one ever noticed or said anything. Why was I so overlooked for so long? What did doctors see, or not see? I will never know the answers. And even if I did, would it just beg more questions? I can only hope my narrative will save another human.

I am not the same person I was at the beginning of this book. I hope you are not either. I hope you have tangled yourself in my ivy, traced across my *mycelium*, and plucked a few forget-me-nots. I hope you know it does not matter what your body looks like, weighs, what color you are, who you love, or where you come from—you deserve good and decent medical care and you should never be afraid to speak up and advocate for yourself until you get it. I know that part is scary. I know that part is hard. But trust me when I say, no one is going to do it for you better than *you* doing it for you. Use your voice. You have it for a reason. Never be afraid to make lists ahead of your appointment, ask follow-up questions, request things be put down or taken out of your record, or switch doctors if you are uncomfortable. I know for many of us, healthcare is a luxury, and the fact that I have written that sentence is an abomination.

You, my dearest reader, are not a waste of space. If you are sick or disabled, chronically ill, any variation of that, you are so valued and you are the bravest among us all. The world is not built for us and yet we must persist and exist anyway. All of this is true.

I will exist here in my space, filled with rage and love and pain and hope. Right now it is all that I can do and it is enough. It will have to be enough. Did you like my story? What did you take away? I hope it haunts you, in the best way.

Entropy

My child is running. I cannot run after her.

But I will walk. For as long as I can.

"And somewhere out there beneath pines and stars,
a ghost of me is chopping mushrooms and
crushing boyensberries into wildwood soup
wondering if magic is real and if I will ever feel safe.

I want to tell her yes. "

Entropy

Thank you to all my hearts.

I love you more than love.

No one and nothing can take that from us.

245

Entropy

Ravven White is a nonbinary femme that originated millions of years ago birthed from unholy swamp gas and the unfettered cries of men. These most recent of days, they operate as a writer, botanical philosopher, artist, and chronic illness navigator. Ravven runs Curious Corvid Publishing (The Sentimental Dead; Haunted Hallways), records her health and trauma journey through Ko-fi and Potions & Processing, their YouTube channel, and haunts the forests and local indie coffee houses. She lives in a castle by the sea with her partner, familiar. their hellhounds, and various familiars. You can find her active on Instagram @ravven_white

Entropy